THE ART OF PARENTING

The Art of Parenting

HOW TO PARENT FROM INFANCY TO ADULTHOOD

K.C. DREISBACH, LMFT

Krystal Dreisbach, Licensed Marriage and Family Therapist, Inc

This publication contains the opinions and ideas of its author. It is intended to provide helpful and informative material on the subjects addressed in the publication. It is sold with the understanding that the author and publisher are not engaged in rendering medical, health, or any other kind of personal professional services in the book. The reader should consult his or her medical, health, or other competent professional before adopting any of the suggestions in this book or drawing inferences from it.

The author and publisher specifically disclaim all responsibility for any liability, loss, or risk, personal or otherwise, which is incurred as a consequence, directly or indirectly, of the use and application of any of the contents of this book.

The names and identifying characteristics of the children, adults, and families mentioned herein have been changed to maintain their confidentiality and privacy.

Copyright © 2021 by Krystal Dreisbach, Licensed Marriage and Family Therapist, Inc

All rights reserved. No part of this book may be reproduced in any manner whatsoever without written permission except in the case of brief quotations embodied in critical articles and reviews. For information, please contact the author at kcdreisbach.com

First Printing, 2021

If you are interested in bringing the author to your live event, contact the author at kcdreisbach.com.

ISBN: 978-0-578-73985-4
ISBN: 978-0-578-73986-1 (ebook)

This one's for you, Papi. I listened to
your lectures, and I
didn't forget them. A girl couldn't ask
for a better father.

Contents

Acknowledgments		xiii
Introduction: Becoming The Best Parent You Can Be!		1
1	Wholistic Parenting	6
2	Developing Your Parenting Philosophy	17
3	Understanding the Parent-Child Relationship	29
4	Understanding Your Parenting Self	39
5	Your Parent-Child Relationship & How to Improve It	58
6	Understanding Psychosocial Development in Children	75
7	Understanding Emotions & Behavior in Children	84
8	Emotion Regulation	94
9	A Wholistic Approach to Discipline	121

10	Co-Parenting	157
11	Parenting & Marriage	165
12	Managing Parental Burnout	180
13	Becoming a Wholistic Parent	192

Appendix A	201
Appendix B	203
Glossary	207
References	217
More by K.C. Dreisbach	221
About The Author	223

This is where parenting as an acquired art comes in.

ALICIA F. LIEBERMAN

Acknowledgments

Writing a book is never easy. It takes much time, dedication, and commitment to make it happen. Although this is my third book, I find myself having several people to thank. I'll keep it brief.

Thank you to Kassandra for all her hard work toward making this book happen. She put in long hours to ensure a quality read. She has always been willing to provide honest feedback, fabulous suggestions, and much of her valuable time.

Thank you to my husband who listened to me for hours upon hours, discussing the various topics in this book, helping me to choose book covers, and just being patient and supportive of my dreams.

To my own parents, who never realized just how brilliant their own parenting was. When I became a therapist and began my career as a relational expert, I was shocked to see that my parents nailed it in so many ways. Their support is invaluable, and their love has always been there.

And finally, to my own children, Richard and Rachel. They are my greatest pride and joy! Thank you, my babies, and remember that I will always love you more than anything else on this earth.

Introduction: Becoming the Best Parent You Can Be!

Welcome to your journey on becoming the best parent that you can be! Wherever you are on your path, congratulations! Parenthood is a rewarding experience filled with moments of pride, joy, and love. I'm going to be honest with you, though, and admit something that most parents don't want to admit to anyone in public:

Parenting (sometimes) just sucks!

Every single parent thinks this at some point in their parenting journey. And they are flat out lying to you if they ever deny it. As a family therapist and a mother of two kids under the age of 8, I can attest to the true horror show that parenting can sometimes be (I once worked with a 16-year-old that caused over $10,000 worth of damage to her family's home!). But does it really have to be that way? Of course not! Although parenting is one of the most challenging gigs around, most parents struggle with it because they have *no clue* what they're doing. They fly from one parental decision to the next with little thought behind the bigger picture of *why* they just made that choice. Every single "Mom Blog," parenting magazine, and parenting book out there is a testament to the hunger that exists for knowledge on the secrets of *how*-to parent.

If you were to search for a parenting book, you'll find thousands of great possibilities, many of which are written by brilliant and exceptional authors, but they all share a similar problem... they're always about the kid! They are all about managing, changing, and manipulating the child into obedience. They all *tell* you *what* to do versus *teach* you *how* to do it.

Here's the problem with that approach: you will know a lot of parenting techniques, but you won't necessarily be a better parent. Think of it this way, does following a recipe make you a chef? Are you suddenly a better cook because you followed the directions in a cookbook? I'm hoping you answered *no*.

If you've done any cooking in your past, you'll know that there's a lot more to being a good cook than just following recipes. There's a certain *art* to it that only experience, skill, and knowledge can provide you. It's through being *taught* the essence of cooking that you truly learn *how* to cook. Essentially, as you learn the *art* of cooking, you *become* a better cook.

And therein lies the problem....

Most of the parenting books you'll find out there today are a recipe. They tell you what ingredients to put into the mix, how long to set the timer, and give you a false impression of what the outcome should look like. (I don't know about you, but my food never looks nearly as pretty or tantalizing as the picture on the recipe.) You might have also noticed that most parenting books are very specific on who they are meant for. You'll find parenting books on parenting babies, parenting toddlers, parenting teenagers, parenting oppositional children, parenting stubborn children, parenting boys, parenting girls, and so on. The list is endless!

Did you ever wonder why this is? Why are all parenting books *so* specific? It's because they are like that cooking recipe. You can't find a dessert recipe that also gives you a chicken dinner. Recipes are very specific because they are intended to produce a very specific outcome. They aren't there to *teach* you *how* to cook. They're there to *tell* you *what* to do so you produce a specific meal.

But what if there was a different way?

What if you could find a parenting book that actually *taught* you *how* to parent? A book that *taught* you the skills behind parenting so that you could parent your child regardless of whether they were a toddler, a teenager, a boy, a girl, and so on? A book that *taught* you the *art* of parenting?

You just might have found that book....

This book is going to lay down the groundwork and foundation for successful parenting throughout your child's lifespan. It is purposefully written to be adaptable to children of any age, gender, or temperament, making this text unique in its approach as a parenting book. I take a wholistic approach to parenting that focuses on the emotional growth and empowerment of the parent versus solely dissecting the child and listing out disciplinary tools.

My goal is to grow *you*, as a parent, so that you can learn the fine art that is parenting. I want *you* to become more knowledgeable about your child's development, to develop the skills you need to create a healthy and positive family environment, and to guide *you* on a journey of self-discovery. Through this process of self-growth, you will not only learn to raise happier and emotionally-healthier children, but you will also grow and develop a deeper, more meaningful sense of purpose as you learn the fine art of parenting. Essentially, parents will be taught *how* to become a *better* parent for a lifetime of family joy and fulfillment.

But why should you trust me?

It can be hard to trust someone you've never met before and know nothing about. Let me help ease some of your hesitations. As mentioned previously, I am a licensed marriage and family therapist, specializing in parenting and working with troubled youth. Over the course of my career, not only have I successfully treated and worked with thousands of children and families in family therapy, I've also taught parenting classes to low-income families, have lectured to graduate students for the past 3 years on topics involving the care and parenting of foster youth, and have provided seminars to various school districts on the psycho-social development of youth to help teachers better understand their students. For years I've served as a Clinical Supervisor in non-profit agencies to help teach and develop new mental health therapists and ensure the quality of care they provide to families. Furthermore, for the past several years, I've shared my parenting expertise through freelance writing as a guest blogger for various popular parenting blogs, and I write regular articles on various parenting topics through my own website.

Most importantly, I am a real mom of two kids, living the day-to-day struggles that every modern parent is dealing with. In my work with families, it is my genuineness and honesty, combined with my clinical knowledge and expertise, that has allowed me to reach and work so effectively with families of varying backgrounds.

As a professional in the field of working with parents and their children, I have seen firsthand the need for a book that is about the *growth* of the parent versus the *raising* of the child. *This* is that book. This unique approach allows me to help you create a loving and structured foundation for your family that you can use no matter how old your child is or what difficulties your child may be facing. This approach will effectively bridge the gap between *telling* you *what* to do and *teaching* you *how* to do it. Get ready to grow as a parent and effectively learn the **Art of Parenting.**

Parenting is my passion. Growing families in love, unity, and emotional health is my vision. Helping parents learn, understand, and apply the art of parenting is my mission.

Are *you* ready?

1

Wholistic Parenting

I've been a therapist for a long time, and for the length of my entire career, my focus has been on working with families. When I became a mother myself, I applied what I had learned as a therapist to my role as a parent. Essentially, I was making sure that I was "walking the walk" and not just "talking the talk." That was extremely important to me. Not only because I wanted to make sure my children were successful or because I knew that these techniques worked, but because I firmly believed that whatever I asked of my clients, I had to be willing to do myself.

Over the years, I received fabulous mentorship from amazing marriage & family therapists. I worked closely with those who specialized in family dynamics and human connection, and I watched as what I learned transformed lives. Then, I used the same techniques for my own family, and I got to enjoy the fruits of that hard labor as my own children (though still small) received compliment after compliment, and acknowledgement after acknowledgement for their behavior. Not just for their behavior, for their kindness, their compassion towards others, and for their bright personalities and sunny dispositions. Of course, they make mistakes. By no means are they perfect... no one is! It's about how they handle their errors and grow from them that really make them shine.

So, what's the secret? What is it that I learned from experts, taught to my clients, and practiced with my own children that made all the difference?

The reality is that it's not magic (but you knew that already), and it's not a special kind of disciplinary technique that you apply or specific way you talk to your kids, or anything like that. Don't get me wrong, all those things are useful and *do* help, but this is a bigger, broader thing we are going to talk about.

See, parenting is incredibly hard. Not just because it's a 24/7 kind of job, but because it's incredibly complex. It's like an onion in many ways, with layer after layer of things that you must keep in mind all of the time. I liken it to spinning plates. Have you ever seen an image like that? A guy spinning a bunch of plates on sticks? Parenting is just like that, and here's why....

Each plate is a component to the parenting job that you must keep in mind, but you must keep every single plate in mind 100% of the time. If you don't, that's how you accidentally drop one. And when one falls, another one is likely to drop too. That's parenting in a nutshell!

This is why there are hundreds (even thousands) of parenting books out there and none of them solve every family's problem. It's not because those books aren't helpful or because they're wrong. In fact, many of those books are incredibly helpful and spot on! I recommend many of them in my work with families.

The reason why is because each of those books are only looking at one of those spinning plates, maybe even a few of those plates, but certainly not all of them. What's more, those books aren't helping parents to learn what all those spinning plates even are!

Think about it... how can you keep track of something when you aren't even aware that it exists? How are you going to be held responsible for something when no one told you that was one of your responsibilities?

Parenting is more than just a slew of parenting techniques or knowing how to "talk to your kids." Each one of those things is a layer to the onion or one of those spinning plates. And you can be a master at those things and still find your family struggling!

So, what do you do? How do you figure this out? You want to be a good parent, right? We all do! But where do you even start? Well... you start by gaining awareness.

1.1 Awareness to Wholistic Parenting

The term "wholistic" (or "holistic") might sound familiar. If you googled this term, you'd end up with the following definition from *Grammarist*:

> ***Wholistic*** *is the philosophy that all parts of a thing are interconnected. In medicine, wholistic treatment is the treatment of a person as a whole, mind, body and social factors.*

This is the missing link. This is the piece that I spent so many years observing, so many years teaching, and practice in my own home. It's this idea of being wholistic, of considering the mind, body, and social environment of my family and shaping my parenting to those factors. Those are the spinning plates, the multiple layers that impact your ability to be an effective parent. It's what I've come to call **Wholistic Parenting**.

When you become a Wholistic Parent, you become knowledgeable of each one of those spinning plates. Since you have this knowledge, you can seek out and acquire parenting techniques that make sense for you and your family. You can adapt different techniques to make them fit your parenting needs, and you are able to take life's curve balls with more grace and calm. This is the value of taking a Wholistic Parenting approach.

Today, I'm going to introduce you to Wholistic Parenting by mapping out all the pieces that comprise of the mind, body, and environment for you and your family. Essentially, I'm going to help you see each of those layers on that onion, each of those spinning plates, so you have a greater awareness of what being a parent is *really* all about.

1.2 Breaking Down Wholistic Parenting

I would be lying if I were to say that Wholistic Parenting is easy- it isn't. There are so many parts that it can feel a little overwhelming. To help us better capture what Wholistic Parenting is all about, I created a map to reference as we break down all the layers. Look at this map now. You can find it at the back of the book in Appendix A.

It's a lot, right? You probably don't even know what you are looking at, and who could blame you? When I broke it all down myself, I went through many iterations of it. Eventually, I landed on this. I'm willing to accept that it's not perfect by any means, but I think it's the closest thing out there to truly mapping out all the pieces that go into parenting. Thus, this is a picture of Wholistic Parenting.

Now that we have an idea of what this encompasses, let's take a closer look and break it down.

The 3 Main Branches

To begin, we'll start by looking at those 3 main branches. Those are the 3 main components that everything else will stem from. They are:

1. **Familial Environment-** This is your home and the multiple parts that go with it.
2. **Social Environment-** This is the outside world that your family lives in. It consists of your neighborhood, social networks, country, and current events.

3. **Child-** This is your child and the unique parts about them that you'll need to keep in mind as you work to parent this person.

These are the big heavy hitters, and when you are parenting, these are the 3 big pieces that are going to affect you and your effectiveness as a parent. You'll need to keep these 3 spinning plates in mind in order to do this job to the best of your ability.

Familial Environment
When we look at the Familial Environment, we can see that it is further broken down into an additional 3 parts. They consist of:

- Parent
- Discipline
- Family Narrative

Hopefully, it makes sense that the family environment would be further broken down into these pieces. Each one of these components are broken down further into more detail. The first one is **Parent**. As the parent, there are many factors that will affect your parenting, including your:

- Physical Health
- Emotional/Mental Health
- Spiritual Health (if applicable to you)
- Knowledge about Parenting

- Skill Set (related to parenting)
- Time (or lack thereof)

These are all layers that affect you as a person. Anything that affects you, is going to affect your family. As such, it's a BIG part of the Familial Environment.

Next is **Discipline**. This one doesn't have as many pieces, but it's still an incredibly important factor to effective parenting. The 3 components that make up Discipline include:

- Rules & Healthy Boundaries
- Structure & Routine
- Rewards & Consequences

These 3 parts are very much interwoven. They must be considered individually but executed as a solid unit. Trust me, that's incredibly hard to do! But it's possible. All it takes is practice. We will be digging deep into discipline in chapter 9.

Finally, you have the **Family Narrative**. This is a big concept but, essentially, it's your family's story. I'll explain it further in chapter 5 and again in chapter 11.

The Family Narrative is further broken down into 2 parts that consist of:

- Ethnic Culture
- Parent-Child Relationship

Your **Ethnic Culture** is going to be a part of your family's story and is, essentially, your family's ethnicity. It impacts everything about you, from how you dress and speak, to the foods you eat, and even how you interact with others.

Your **Parent-Child Relationship** is essentially the bond you have with your child. I further broke down this concept into 3 more factors:

- Healthy Boundaries
- Quality Time
- Warmth, Love, & Attunement

In chapter 3, we will dive into the Parent-Child relationship with much more depth. You'll develop a deeper understanding of attachment styles, which impacts your boundaries with your child, as well as how you attune with them. Then, in chapter 5, you'll learn more about the parent-child relationship and quality time.

Social Environment

When we look at the **Social Environment**, we can see there are 3 parts to it. It consists of:

- Social Culture
- Current Events
- Social Influence

Social Culture is similar to ethnic culture, but also different. Let's say you are Cuban, and this is your Ethnic Culture. If you live in Cuba, it will also be your Social Culture. If you live in the United States, however, this is no longer your Social

Culture. Your Social Culture now becomes that of the area in which you live. As such, your Social Culture is subject to change depending on where your family currently resides.

Current Events greatly impact your parenting, whether you like it or not. If you live in an active war zone, that will cause you to be more protective, fearful, and anxious. This will certainly change what you allow your children to do daily. This is an extreme example, but it effectively demonstrates how current events will contribute to your parenting. Over examples might be government elections, pandemics, natural disasters, or civil unrest.

Social Influence consists of the people that might influence you or your child. Right now, I might be a social influence on you, which might cause a shift in how you parent. Your child's peers are a social influence on them, which may cause them to behave in ways you approve or disapprove of. Other social influences include neighbors, the media, and extended family among other things.

The Child

Hopefully, it makes sense that your child would be further broken down into multiple parts, just like you were as the parent. Those pieces include your child's:

- Physical Health
- Emotional/Mental Health
- Spiritual Health (if applicable to them)
- Developmental Age

- Sibling Position

These are all layers that affect your child as a person. And anything that affects your child, is going to affect how he behaves, which will then affect how you respond to him. As such, it's a BIG part of Wholistic Parenting.

1.3 Where Do We Go from Here?

Hopefully, this first chapter provided you with a basic understanding of Wholistic Parenting. It can be overwhelming, I know, but awareness of all the parts helps you better understand how one thing impacts another. Families are systems, with many moving parts. Focusing on only one part of the system does little in helping you understand how each piece connects and affects the other. Only after understanding the greater picture, can you begin to hone in on those smaller pieces that might be broken or need a tune-up.

So, let's talk about a deeper dive into this knowledge. The more you understand all these parts, the better you'll be at spinning all those plates. This is absolutely correct! Knowledge is power! As such, let's talk a little more about how you should use this book.

As I hinted to earlier, Wholistic Parenting has several parts that should be looked at individually but executed as a cohesive unit. I spent many nights contemplating how to write a book that would touch on everything individually but demonstrate the interconnectedness of it all. A lot of the heartache came into structuring the book in a way that made sense. This is what I came up with....

This first chapter is designed to give you that bird's-eye-view, showing you each part separately, while at the same time displaying how each piece is interconnected to the other. Moving forward, the book will jump from one "branch" to the other, as needed, in order to fully discuss each topic. Remember, everything must be executed as a unit because everything is related and connected. This first chapter, however, should give you enough of a foundation of this broader picture while you discuss different pieces within it, keeping you from getting lost.

As you read each chapter, you'll be digging a little deeper and learning more about each branch. By the end of the book, you should have a wholistic understanding of your parenting.

Remember, Wholistic Parenting is the key to successful parenting and a happy, loving, and untied family. It's time to evolve into the best parent that you can be. Let's begin....

2

Developing Your Parenting Philosophy

So, you've turned the page and you're ready to dig in and evolve into a better version of your parenting-self. I'm so glad that you did!

In this chapter, we're going to take a look at parenting philosophies. Specifically, we're going to examine *your* parenting philosophy by helping you understand my own. In this way, you can begin developing the parenting philosophy that will serve as your guide on the journey ahead.

2.1 Why have a Parenting Philosophy?

I told you in the last chapter that this book would discuss the fundamentals to parenting so that you could take what I teach you and apply it to the raising of your child, regardless of age, gender, etc. In order to do that, however, we have to understand the theoretical underpinnings of healthy, effective, and loving parenting.

If you were to look up the word "philosophy" in the Oxford American Dictionary, you would get a few different definitions. One of those definitions would be, "a personal rule of life" or "...the causes and nature of things and of principles governing existence" ("Philosophy," def. 2.b). From these definitions, we can see that the philosophy of something is the most basic component of that subject matter. It is the *foundation* that the subject is built upwards from.

My goal is to help you become a better parent by helping you grow and evolve. Everything needs a solid foundation to be built from. Trees require a strong and dense root structure that keep the tree held high and strong against winds. A house needs a solid foundation to be built upon, or the whole building collapses. Parenting is no different.

Having a parenting philosophy *is* that foundation. It's your fundamental beliefs, concepts, and attitudes that you will use to *root* your future parenting decisions. In many ways, it's the core that you will be able to go back to and rely on when you find yourself unsure of how to proceed in any given parenting dilemma with your child. It will be your compass on your journey.

My Parenting Philosophy- The 7 Key Principles

There are many views on how to approach parenting and discipline. As a therapist, I come from the perspective that there is no right or wrong parenting approach. They all have similarities and differences, strengths and weaknesses. As a therapist, I am fairly eclectic in what I teach my clients, combining various styles and tweaking different techniques to help families with their own unique circumstances. Furthermore, what I preach, I also follow, applying the same techniques to the raising of my own children. As I always tell my clients, "I will not recommend something to you that I wouldn't be willing to do myself."

I'm going to share with you the basic points of my own parenting philosophy, which will create the foundation for our journey together. Consider each one, and if it feels right to you, then feel free to incorporate it as part of your own parenting foundation. If something doesn't feel right, then don't feel pressured to take it. All I ask is that you take the time to consider *why* that point doesn't feel right to you, and then ask that you adapt it to what's best for you and your family.

1. All Parents are Trying Their Very Best

In my work as a therapist, I have come to see that, all parents, regardless of their background, age, religion, etc., are doing the very best that they can. Unfortunately, as parents, we sometimes make choices that may not be the best, and this can cause others to be critical of us as parents. Maybe you've spanked your child, or perhaps you yell a little more often than you would like. This does not mean you are a "bad" parent.

With some exceptions, I believe that parents generally want what is best for their kids. We are biologically wired to want to raise children who are happy, healthy, and well-adjusted. Unfortunately, other things might come in the way of this, such as substance abuse, traumatic past experiences of abuse or neglect, poor modeling from our own parents, mental health issues, or societal pressures and norms that can come to affect how we parent our children. This, in turn, can cause us to make choices that end up harming our own kids.

2. *Parenting is a 24/7 Job*

Parenting is a job, a responsibility, and it is seldom easy. It is a difficult task to undertake the caring and raising of a young human being, and it is a task that should be taken seriously. Although being a parent brings with it a wealth of love, laughter, and joyous moments, it is definitely not for the faint of heart. Part of what makes parenting so difficult, is that it is a 24 hours, 7 days a week kind of job, with no end in sight. Once a parent, you're always a parent. There are no holidays, "breaks," or "end" to your parenting duties and responsibilities. Once you take on being a parent, you must accept that this job will supersede all others, and it is for life. You will never stop being a mother or a father, even when that child is grown with their own children. You are still their parent. Because of this fact, you have to be willing to battle the tantrums, kicking, screaming, and crying of your child at any point of the day. And this is *extremely* tough work!

3. *Your Children Always Come First*

Most folks can buy-in to my first two points, but this one becomes a little harder to swallow. Your children should always come first. No matter how tired you are, how hungry or thirsty, or how sick you feel... your child always comes first. My husband recently told me that there is a new generation of parents that he has dubbed, the "Me Mommy." The "Me Mommy" is a mother (or father for that matter) who is a little more concerned about taking care of his or her own physical/emotional/social needs before that of their children.

Now, I want to tread lightly here because I believe this is a very important point to discuss and understand. As much as I believe that your children should truly come first, I also believe that you must work to find balance. All parents need to take care of themselves too! The reality is, if you physically, mentally, or emotionally fall apart, you will not be able to care for your children. Because of this, your own self-care is vital to the care of your kids! As such, balance is key to this foundational point. You must place the needs of your children before your own, but within reason, and not at the risk of losing your own sanity.

4. There is No Such Thing as a "Bad" Kid

Evil, "bad" children just don't exist. You *must* believe that your child is inherently *good*, or at the very least *neutral*. Children who do "bad things" are *not* bad children. There are many reasons why a child may engage in rotten behavior, but none of these reasons stem from the child being simply a "bad seed." You must be able to understand and accept this point. Too often, I have heard parents state, "They're just a bad kid," when coming to me in therapy for help. As much as I empathize with them, I work to help them understand that this is simply not true. Let's take a moment to think of this critically. If you truly believe you simply birthed a "bad apple," then you will also need to accept that there is *nothing* you can do to change it, and you have *zero* control over the situation. After all, if your child is simply just a "bad kid," and nothing you did (or didn't do) contributed to the problem, then there is nothing you can do now to change it. The "badness" is simply inherent in their DNA. It is their personality.

Now, if I was a parent reading this, it probably wouldn't sit well with me. In fact, I would feel pretty hopeless, annoyed, and probably a little angry too. If you believe, instead, that your child is inherently "good" (or at the very least "neutral"), then you believe that their *behavior* is "bad," not him or her. If you believe their *behavior* is bad, then I will tell you that *behavior* can be changed. Throughout this book, you will learn the fundamental points you will need to begin changing "bad" behavior into "good." And you will see that there is no such thing as a "bad kid," just kids with unsavory behaviors.

5. As a Parent, Your Primary Role is to be Your Child's Teacher, Not Their Friend

So often I hear parents telling me that they want to be "friends" with their kids. They want to be the "cool" mom/dad. This, in turn, changes the power differential of the Parent-Child Relationship, and sets it up for failure. As a parent, you need to understand that your primary role in that child's life is to be their first and most prominent teacher, not their friend. From the very beginning of that child's life, you will be teaching them everything they need to know about living a successful life as a productive citizen of your culture and society. From morality and ethical standards, to basic social customs, to how to clean their rooms, your lessons will be the most deeply ingrained teachings in their conscious and subconscious minds. And the most important medium you will use to impart these lessons is the Parent-Child Relationship. Always remember, you are the parent; the neighbor kid is their friend.

6. *YOU Are the Parent, and Thus, YOU Set the Rules*

This point goes hand-in-hand with the one just mentioned. When we treat our children like our friends, we give them more authority by elevating them into a place of parental power. Think of it this way, when you go out with a friend, you both might debate about where to go out, who will drive, what movie you might see, etc. You are both friends, so you both have an equal "say" in what is going to occur on your outing. This is not the case with you and your child. You may offer your child options on where to go or what movie to see, but typically the options that you provide have been narrowed down to those that you feel are appropriate for you, your child, and your wallet. Why do you do this? Because YOU are the parent and YOU set the rules. In therapy, it is very common for me to encounter parents who make the mistake of elevating their child into a place of parental power. For example, let's look at a child who has a curfew of 7:00 p.m. The child whines and complains that "All of my friends get to stay out late," and begs to stay out much later. The parent sighs and agrees to let the child stay out. Why? Why might a parent do this? Take a moment to consider your own behavior as a parent. Reasons may include:

- Not wanting to disappoint the child
- A desire to be a "cool" parent
- To be loved and liked by the child (If you can admit this one, good for you!)

Making this decision based off any of the reasons listed above is a poor choice (more on this later) and can be more problematic if this is a two-parent household. It is critical that in a two-parent household parents approach decision making as a team. One parent should avoid making parental decisions (especially BIG ones) without involving the other parent. Failure to include the second parent in decision making can create a problematic dynamic known as "triangulation." In order to help us understand this phenomenon a little better, notice the below graphic. This Parent-Child Relational Triangle depicts the parental relationship with the child in the appropriate way:

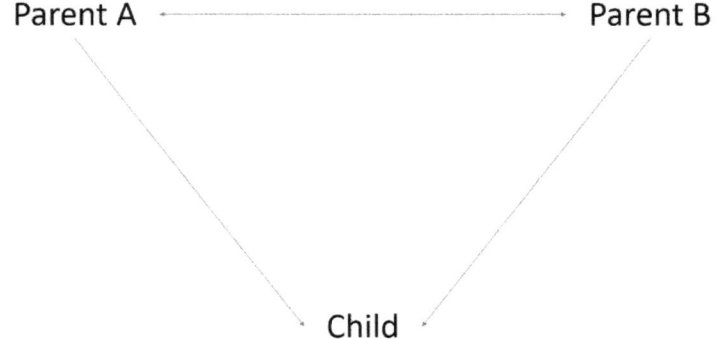

In this graphic, both parents are placed at the top, with equal authority. Rules of the home and parenting are done together, with open communication between both parents. This is depicted by the double-sided arrow. The authority of both of these parents flow downward toward the child in an equal way. Both parents have equal authority over the raising, praising, and disciplining of the child.

Alternatively, in a situation where the child has been elevated to a place of parental authority, our Parent-Child Relational Triangle looks more like this:

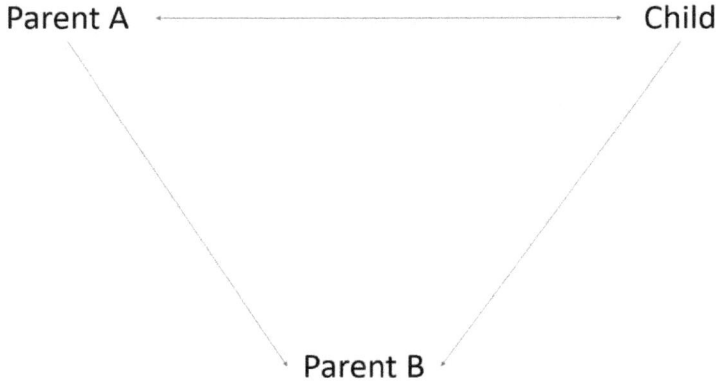

In this diagram, we see that Parent A and the Child share authority with one another (i.e. the double-sided arrow) while the "parental power" for Parent B has been removed (i.e. both arrows point downward toward Parent B). This, in turn, renders Parent B's authority null-and-void. This sets up an erroneous power dynamic in the household. It's a simple enough concept to understand, but most parents would adamantly disagree that they've ever engaged in this second relational pattern. You might even be thinking that right now.

Regardless of whether or not you've engaged in this relational pattern, it might surprise you to learn that it is incredibly easy to accidentally slip into this kind of power dynamic. And in truth, we all engage in this type of pattern from time to time. This occasional slip is not a big deal, but the more your family slips into this pattern, the more common it becomes. Then, in some families, this ends up becoming the "norm" in the Parent-Child Relationship. Regardless of what the situation is for your family, always remember that *authority* must flow from the parents down to the child. With that said, however, this is not a dictatorship! Don't be a parental tyrant!

7. The Core of the Parent-Child Relationship MUST be in Respect

Your child must respect you and YOU must respect your child. When working with families, I've met with folks who mistakenly think of *respect* and *parental authority* as interchangeable concepts. As such they end up treating their children without respect. From the first day of your child's life, you should treat that baby with respect. Respect needs to be at the core of your relationship with your child. This, in turn, will help create a dynamic where your child respects you too. In all truth, respect should be the cornerstone of your household. Both parents and all children in the home should demonstrate respect to one another. As previously mentioned, some folks mistake respect for authority, elevating their child to a place of parental authority in order to demonstrate "respect" to their child. *Respect* and *authority* are not interchangeable concepts, but they are also not mutually exclusive of one another. They frequently go hand-in-hand. The key to remember is that you do not need to have "authority" in any given situation in order to demand "respect." Think of it this way, if you are an employee, you deserve respect, right? Your supervisor can treat you with respect and dignity, regardless of the fact that authority flows down from them to you. The same can be achieved in your household.

Now, in this same vein, let's talk about respect toward your co-parent. Remember how I stated that parents will *accidentally* raise their child to a place of parental authority, and thus, lower the second parent's (i.e. Parent B) parental authority? One of the ways that this easily occurs in families, without anyone really even realizing it, is by treating your co-parent in a way that shows disrespect to that parent. Perhaps you yell at them in front of the children, or say something smug, such as, "You never remember anything," or maybe you even call them a name (i.e. "You're such an idiot"). All of these interactions demonstrate disrespect to your parenting partner. When this is done in front of your child, it sends an unspoken message to your child that you and your co-parent do not share equal parental authority. Furthermore, if you engage with your partner in this way because of something your child told you (i.e. *"Did you forget to give our son a jacket?!? He says you didn't give him one. How could you forget to do that?! You always forget everything!"*), you have now elevated your child into a place of authority, above your co-parent. We will talk more about this point in the coming chapters since it is so important when we talk about co-parenting.

2.2 Where Do You Go from Here?

If you agree with these seven principles, then I think you will really enjoy what this book has to offer. If you found some points didn't settle well with you, that's ok too! Take that information and create your own parenting philosophy that feels right to you. As we move through each chapter, I will refer back to these principles since we will rely on them in order to successfully implement many of our future parenting concepts and techniques. You will also notice that I will share many stories with you of the real-life experiences of cases I have worked with, as well as some of my own. I think it is important for parents to hear the struggles that other moms and dads face every day with raising their own kids. As parents, we need to support one another, and help each other, in raising the next generation of our society to the best of our ability. Finally, I do try to keep gender in mind as I write, referring to gender-neutral terms, such as "parent" throughout the book. To keep the flow of writing, and to avoid overuse of these gender-neutral terms, please realize that I may refer to terms like *mother, father, dad, etc.* Recognize that this is not done to only reference one gender, but rather, to keep the writing of this book from being bogged down. At any time that I say "dad," it could (and should) be easily switched in your mind to "mom" and vice versa. In this way, these stories and techniques better reflect you and your current parenting situation.

＃ 3

Understanding the Parent-Child Relationship

So, now that we have discussed the seven principles of my parenting philosophy, it's time to understand, *"What is the parent-child relationship?"* Quite simply, the **Parent-Child Relationship** is the bond or connection that a parent has to their child and that the child has to their parent. Another word we can use to talk about the parent-child relationship is *attachment*. In the field of psychology, **attachment** is defined as a mutual, long-standing bond between two people (particularly between a caregiver and infant) that defines the quality of the relationship (Papalia and Feldman 213). As we move through this chapter, we'll be using *attachment* and *Parent-Child relationship* interchangeably.

Now that we know what the Parent-Child relationship is, let's talk about when it begins developing. Essentially, the parent-child relationship starts from the moment of birth. Some people might even argue that it starts as early as conception, when parents become aware that they have a new child on the way. The reason why some folks may argue that attachment begins at conception is because, frequently, parents may begin to feel "attached" to the child this early on in the pregnancy. Parents may sing to this developing baby, they may read stories, the parent may begin talking to the child, etc. What research has shown is that, in the womb, the child will begin to recognize their parents' voices. If you think about it, this is amazing, to think that from the moment that child has the ability to hear, you can begin developing a relationship with this young person.

Regardless of whether or not you believe that attachment can begin while the child is still in the womb, attachment *does* begin to form once the child is born, and it continues to develop throughout the lifespan of the child and parent. The question now may become, how do you develop this relationship? How do you start to form a positive connection with this child so that your future parenting relationship with this young human being is a positive and successful one?

The answer is much simpler than you might think, and the reality is that it's not that tricky either. The simple fact is attachment is formed by the little interactions that you have with your child. Everything counts! Big or small, everything you do from singing your child to sleep at night, to feeding them when they're hungry, to changing their diapers when they're dirty, to kissing their ouchies and owies, contributes to the Parent-Child relationship in a way that is either going to make it positive or negative.

The interesting thing about attachment is that there are "styles" of attaching. Through research, psychologists have come to identify four basic attachment styles. As the parents of our children, we have our own attachment style that we have developed over time. This style began when we were born via the way we attached with our own parents. Furthermore, our children will have their own attachment style, which will be shaped by the way we interact with them in their early developing years.

There are a lot of things that go into attachment and the type of attachment style your child will have. Some of these things will be more biologically based, such as their personality and their temperament. Some of it will be molded by the interactions they have with you. Essentially, what we're looking at is a combination. Now, there has been a lot of debate in the psychological community about whether "parenting" or a child's "biology" is the most important component on how a person ends up in life. The debate is usually referred to as **nature vs nurture**. But this debate has finally come to rest with the understanding that both parts play a significant role. John Santrock explained this issue, stating research has shown that all people are a mix of their nature (i.e. their genetic make-up) and nurture (i.e. the environment they grew up in and the care they received). Our genetics, in combination with how we were raised and our past experiences shapes and defines everything about us. This includes our development, how we interact with people, and the way we form relational bonds with others (125).

So, although your child's biology is going to be a large component of who they are, your parenting can dramatically shape and mold it.

There are four types of attachment styles that your child can develop, and they are *Secure, Avoidant, Ambivalent,* and *Disorganized/Disoriented*. Papalia and Feldman defined these four styles as follows:

- **Secure Attachment-** When an infant is able to to find comfort from their caregiver easily and effectively in the face of a stressful situation (214)
- **Avoidant Attachment-** A pattern of behavior where an infant rarely cries or fusses when they are separated from a caregiver, and then avoids contact or interaction with this caregiver when he/she returns to the infant (214)
- **Ambivalent/Resistant Attachment-** When an infant shows distress before a caregiver leaves them, then is significantly upset while the caregiver is absent, and then wants *and* resists contact with their caregiver when the caregiver returns (214)
- **Disorganized/Disoriented Attachment-** In this behavioral pattern, an infant (after being left alone by the caregiver) will show different, contradictory behaviors when the caregiver returns (214)

Your goal as a parent is for your child to develop secure attachment. The reason why is because *secure attachment* essentially reflects a sense of trust from your child. Securely attached children have learned that they can trust their caregivers, and they can trust their own ability to get their needs met.

3.1 The Importance of a Secure Attachment Style

There are a lot of benefits to a child having a secure attachment to their caregivers, and this is part of the reason why you want to work so hard to make sure you develop a very positive and nourishing Parent-Child Relationship. Research has shown that children who have secure attachment to a nurturing adult are better able to develop healthy relationships in the future. Furthermore, the relationships that they form with their future spouse, with peers, and with other family members are more positive and more likely to be relationships that are beneficial to the child. These kids also have an increased likelihood to have a higher self-esteem and self-image, and they tend to be more confident in their interactions with their peers and with the world at large. Other benefits include a more varied vocabulary, increased curiosity about the world, increased empathy, more resilience to hardships, and they are better able to get along with their peers. Moreover, children who are securely attached tend to interact more appropriately with teachers and other authority figures. Finally, in adolescence, these children who have developed that positive Parent-Child Relationship are individuals who are more likely to have stable friendships, less hostility, and less problematic behaviors.

By contrast, the other attachment styles can actually contribute to mental health disorders. An example might be Reactive Attachment Disorder, where children struggle to form positive relationships with people. Children with this disorder also tend to engage in behaviors that are considered risky or dangerous to themselves and other people. Even if your child doesn't develop a mental health condition due to their poor attachment, they can still form maladaptive behaviors that can be stressful to deal with as a parent. You could have a child who is overly clingy and struggles to self soothe. These kids can also be more hostile or more aggressive with peers, which can lead to issues when they go to daycare or begin attending school. As teenagers, they struggle to form intimate relationships that are appropriate with their peers and/or significant others. Given this information, it is easy to see how it is in your best interest to work on building a healthy attachment with your child, beginning in infancy. If you find yourself in a situation where your relationship with your child appears to already be damaged, then it would behoove you to begin working on repairing that damaged relationship to the best of your ability. We will discuss this more in chapter 5.

3.2 Developing Secure Attachment in Children

Now that we have learned how important it is for your child to develop a healthy and secure attachment style, let's talk about how we can help create that positive Parent-Child Relationship from the very beginning. To begin this discussion, let's start with the obvious: How do you help your child learn to trust you? The answer is simple: You meet their needs.

During infancy when your child is hungry, you feed them. When your child needs a diaper change, you change it promptly. When your child is cold, you warm them up with blankets or warm clothing. When your child is hot, you take off layers of clothing and seek to cool them down in some way. All of these actions that you naturally do as a parent help to develop this secure and positive attachment. These actions start to show your child that *you* can be trusted, that *adults* can be trusted, and that the *world* is not a scary and dangerous place. This, in turn, allows for your child to feel confident about the world they live in, and for them to feel safe enough to explore it. Lacking this kind of interaction with your child creates mistrust, which then results in the previously listed, problematic attachment styles (i.e. *Avoidant, Ambivalent,* and *Disorganized/Disoriented*). These actions that you take as a parent in the care of your baby or child are the obvious ones. So, let's talk about what's *not* so obvious.

In order to help your child develop a positive Parent-Child relationship with you, and a healthy secure attachment style, you must also meet your child's emotional needs. Although this may seem very obvious to most parents, you would be surprised how many parents aren't aware of this and/or don't know *how* to meet their child's emotional needs. Meeting your child's emotional needs can be more important than meeting their physical needs, such as their need for food and drink. This is a strong statement to make, but failure to meet a child's emotional needs can have longer, more impactful negative consequences for a child.

Back in 1958, Harry Harlow began studying how monkeys bond with their mothers because he wanted to understand how human infants develop attachment to their parents. He was particularly interested in knowing what was the basis of the emotional bond that they form. Early attachment theorists had stated that a child attaches to his mother because the mother is the one who provides him with food via breastfeeding. This was a very behavioral, biologically based theory that many researchers believed created attachment (i.e. *behavioral theory of attachment*). Harlow didn't buy into this idea, however. He believed that attachment was developed as a result of the mother providing "tactile comfort" to the infant. He believed that infants had an innate need to be touched and to be held by their caregiver for emotional comfort.

Harlow had several experiments that he conducted using young monkeys in order to study his theory of attachment. Probably one of his most famous studies was one where he provided infant monkeys with surrogate mothers. In this study, he took eight monkeys and had them separated from their moms immediately after birth. These monkeys were placed in cages with two surrogate mothers, one that was made completely of wire and one that was covered in a soft terry cloth material. Over the course of 165 days, these monkeys were studied. Four of the monkeys were able to gain milk from the Wire Mother, and four of these monkeys were able to gain milk from the Cloth Mother. The results of the study showed that all eight monkeys spent more time with, and appeared to prefer, the Cloth Mother over the Wire Mother, regardless of whether or not the Cloth Mother was able to provide the baby with milk. The baby monkeys would only go to the Wire Mother when they were hungry. Once they were full, they would travel back to the Cloth Mother. If something frightening was placed in the cage with the four monkeys, the babies would seek out the Cloth Mother for comfort and refuge. The results of this study supported a new, revolutionary theory of attachment, in which it was theorized that the sensitive responses and sense of security given by a caregiver is the larger, more important factor of attachment.

If your child has one of the other attachment styles, such as *avoidant* or *disorganized*, they are not lost and gone forever! Your ability to parent your child effectively, and in a positive way, later on in their life can actually correct these other, more problematic, attachment styles. This is a very important piece of information to remember, because what I'm essentially telling you is that you can't break your child! Just because you were not the best parent when your child was an infant, does not mean that you cannot improve in your parenting and repair damage caused in the past. You can become an amazing parent and still have a healthy Parent-Child relationship with your child.

The main message I want you to take away from this chapter is that a healthy Parent-Child relationship is the key to parenting success. Helping your child develop a Secure Attachment style helps to set your child up for greater success later in life. Finally, damages in the Parent-Child relationship can be remedied. Just because you made a mistake once or twice in how you interacted with your kid, does not mean that you've completely destroyed your relationship with your child. Just like Rome wasn't built in a day, you can't create healthy attachment in a day and you can't destroy it in a day either! Later on in this book, we will be discussing something I call the "Emotional Piggy Bank," which is where you will learn how your interactions with your child affect the relationship you have with them, and how those same interactions will help you build up a positive Parent-Child relationship.

4

Understanding Your Parenting Self

In therapy, I work with folks from all walks of life, from varying cultural identities and religious beliefs, to economic statuses, ages, and so on. It doesn't matter who the client is, or what the problem is, one of the first steps in psychotherapy is to observe and assess the situation, problem, and the person or family. This process allows me to gain an understanding of what it is that the client feels needs to be addressed. It also gives me some insight on how the problem developed over time. But what is the purpose? Quite simply, you can't know where you are going if you don't know where you are starting from.

In order for you to know who you want to be as a parent, you need to first understand who you already are. As much as you might already have a firm grasp of the kind of mom or dad you want to become, have you ever taken the time to assess your progress in achieving that vision? By taking time to honestly determine the parent you are right now, you will be able to better determine the steps you need to take to become the parent you always dreamed you would be.

There are other benefits to this exercise. While in my graduate program, my professor required that all of the students become an "expert" on one therapeutic approach. We learned many different therapeutic models, but before graduating, we had to demonstrate a high level of proficiency in at least one of the approaches. It was a long and tedious journey; one which, at the time, I truly didn't understand the purpose of. I knew that there were several different therapy models I liked, but none that I loved. As such, I couldn't buy-in to the idea of being an "expert" on just *one* model. I challenged her about this requirement and lost the argument, but for a good reason.

There is an extreme benefit to knowing and understanding one therapeutic approach. Therapy is not as clean and linear of a process as one might like it to be. It can get messy, and the messiness can cause treatment to steer off course. When this happens, a therapist needs to "regroup." Because I was expected to become an expert on a specific approach, when I needed to re-evaluate a case, I was able to re-conceptualize the case from this approach. In doing so, I am better able to see what needs to change within the family dynamic, and have several hypotheses on what I can do to make that change a reality.

So why have taken the time to share all of this with you? It's because, in the end, parenting is no different. We all have some semblance of an idea of who we want to be as parents, and we truly try to manage our kids, spouses, and family life in a manner that honors this "perfect parent perception." Reality, however, loves to shove itself in the way, and that *perfect parent* rarely makes an appearance. Things start to get out of hand and a little messy, leaving us feeling flustered, overwhelmed, and burned-out. This is the time to regroup.

Whether you regroup on your own because you are a single parent, or you regroup with your co-parent, you need to push the "pause" button and take a moment to center yourself and figure everything out. This task can be overwhelming, and, at times, you might be left feeling confused on *how* you need to manage the challenge at hand. One of the simplest ways of tackling this problem is to revisit who you currently are as a parent, and who it is that you hope to become. Is your initial reaction/inclination of the situation (i.e. your current parenting self) lining up with your vision of the parent you want to be (i.e. your perfect parent perception)? If it does, then awesome! You are well on your way in this journey. If it doesn't, however, how do they differ? Is there a problem with this difference?

Everyone has a different style and different strategies to parenting. My own parents were quite different, with my dad being fairly strict, protective, and the primary disciplinarian. My mother, by contrast, was much more lenient and less confrontational. In my own household, I tend to be the primary disciplinarian, I am more protective than my husband, and I adhere to my household rules fairly consistently. My husband, on the other hand, I refer to as the "Weak Zebra," because he's a big softy, and my daughter is usually able to convince him to let her do/eat anything! [I call him the Weak Zebra because, in a herd of zebras, the "weak" one is usually the one to get eaten by the lions first (i.e. the children!).]

So, who is the Weak Zebra in your house? Is it you? Who's the primary disciplinarian? Who are YOU as a parent right now?

4.1 The 4 Parenting Styles

To help you on your quest to discover who you are as a mom/dad, it might be helpful to have some understanding of what research has discovered about different parenting styles. Now, I've read many "pop psychology" articles and blog posts out there that tend to over complicate this, adding more parenting styles than is supported by clinical research. Those articles aren't bad, they just add more than there really is to the mix, and I'm not interested in giving you information that isn't supported by research. I wouldn't do that to my clients in the therapy room and I am certainly not going to do that here.

Decades of research have concluded that there are 4 basic parenting styles:

- Permissive/Indulgent
- Authoritative
- Authoritarian
- Neglectful

Permissive (indulgent) is described as parents who allow their children to govern their own activities as much as possible. They give their children much power when it comes to making decisions in the home, and do not discipline their children very often. Papalia and Feldman report that these parents are warm in nature, indulgent, demand little (if anything) from their children, and noncontrolling (301).

Authoritative is described as a parenting style that honors a child's individuality but balances it with social constraints. They implement punishment, when necessary, that is just and fair. These parents demand good behaviors from their children, by maintaining firm standards, but are also loving and accepting (Papalia and Feldman 301).

Authoritarian parenting is characterized by a sense of control and obedience. Authoritarian parents hold their kids to rigid behavioral standards, use punishment frequently, are less warm and more detached in the relationship with their child.

Finally, **Neglectful** is characterized by a lack of involvement. These parents rarely spend quality time with their children (Santrock 77). Parents who fall into this category know little about their children, and they fail to provide structure and/or healthy boundaries for their kids.

For the purposes of this book, we won't be looking at Neglectful Parenting. Chances are, if you're spending time reading this book, you're not a neglectful parent. Most likely, your parenting style will fall into one of the other 3 categories. As such, we are going to leave Neglectful behind and continue by examining the remaining 3 styles.

Now, I like to conceptualize these styles as a continuum, with Permissive to the far left, Authoritarian to the far right, and Authoritative somewhere in the middle:

Permissive ←——————→ Authoritative ←——————→ Authoritarian

You shouldn't think of these styles as a rigid box that you either fit into or don't. You could fall anywhere, which is why I like to teach this topic to my clients as a continuum, where you may be somewhere between Permissive and Authoritative, but perhaps lie closer to the left on the continuum versus the right. Knowing where you lie on this continuum helps you to understand what your "default" settings are when you come up against a parenting problem, or when you are parenting from a place of distress versus from a place of calm and composure.

It should be noted that parents who have more Authoritative parenting styles are more likely to produce children who are better adjusted. Research shows that these kids grow up to be happier, assertive, independent, self-controlled, and have a more exploratory nature (Papalia and Feldman 301). This is in comparison to the children of Authoritarian parents who often are discontented, more rebellious, withdrawn from others, and distrustful; or from the children of Permissive parents, who are more likely to lack self-control, display immaturity, and are the least exploratory in their nature (Papalia and Feldman 301).

The belief that is perpetrated from these findings is that *only* the Authoritative parenting style produces happy kids, and this is simply not the case. We can all think of a *super* Permissive parent who has adult children that are quite successful, and vice versa. There are many reasons for this to occur, but one of the reasons has to do with "goodness of fit," which we will jump into a little further along in this chapter.

At this point, I would like you to take a moment to determine where you land on the parenting continuum. Try to be honest with yourself... there's no one else watching, and no one else knows what I'm asking you to do. Don't try to defend or explain your answer either. This is just a private reflection for yourself. Having an honest opinion of where you are on that continuum allows you to understand further who you are as a parent. It will also give you more insight into your "default" parenting mode when faced with a parenting-related dilemma or when stressed. Once you have a firm grasp of that, you can begin to determine what new habits you will need to develop in order to increase your chances of reaching your perfect parenting vision.

4.2 The Unique Components of the Parenting You

Now that you have learned about the 3 parenting styles (excluding Neglectful) and have, hopefully, determined where you lie on the parenting continuum, we can begin looking at the other variables that affect your parenting. There are 6 components that affect you and how you parent:

- Your Default Parenting Style
- Past Experiences
- Your Self-Esteem/ Self-Image
- Your Emotional Wellbeing/ Mental Health
- Your Personality
- Your Co-Parent

With the exception of the first one, we will go through each one in a little more depth so that you can understand how these differing items affect you and how you parent. One thing you will notice is that many things will intertwine and affect something else. This is an important notion to remember, because all parenting is this way. As we work through this book, you will see how everything is connected, and how rarely the answer to solving behavioral issues with children is rarely working with the child alone. Most times, the family is key, with much of the work being done with the parent.

Past Experiences

Your past experiences will affect you and who you are as a parent. I think this is a fairly obvious point that you most likely already know, but it is an important one nonetheless. Understanding *how* it is that your past is coming in to play a part in who you are now is part of knowing where you've been. In therapy, I frequently teach individuals that understanding the "why" of something can help in identifying what needs to change.

Most fundamentally, a huge component of your past experience is the way you, yourself, were raised. How your parents raised you is going to dictate a lot about how you will raise your own children. How many times have you caught yourself saying, "OMG! I sound *just* like my mom right now!" Probably more times than you care to admit. And that's ok too! It's completely normal and natural for you to parent similarly to how your parents did. Your parents acted as your role model for what "parenting" looks like, whether for good or bad. As such, your parenting style is going to be very similar to theirs.

Similarly, your attachment style to your own children has been largely affected by the way your parents interacted with you as an infant. Take a moment to reflect our discussion on attachment and the Parent-Child relationship in the previous chapter. That chapter taught you how your interactions with your baby and young children created the foundation of your Parent-Child relationship. The same is true for you too, with your own parents. The attachment that you developed with them set the stage for how you treat your own kids, and thus, affecting the type of attachment you have developed.

Trauma is another major factor that will affect your parenting. Whether the trauma was physical abuse, sexual abuse, emotional/mental abuse, witnessing traumatic events (such as a death), or being involved in a natural disaster (such as a hurricane or flood), these past experiences have lasting effects on the human psyche. For example, I had a client once who experienced sexual abuse as a young girl, which haunted her into her adult years. When she gave birth to her first baby, she had every hope of breastfeeding. The moment the child was placed on the breast, however, she felt a large sense of anxiety and had to pull the baby off. She tried many times to breastfeed the baby again, but every time, she became very anxious, affecting her milk supply and making breastfeeding a miserable experience for her. She struggled to determine *why* breastfeeding was so provoking for her, but after a few sessions of therapy, she was able to determine that the sensations of breastfeeding served as a trigger and reminder of her past sexual abuse.

Trauma doesn't have to be a major life event to affect someone's daily life. Every day, seemingly ordinary experiences can create trauma reactions in people, and affect your parenting. A dog bite as a child can cause you to be jumpy with stray dogs, and thus, can leave you acting overly cautious when your child wants to pet the puppies at the local pet store. An unfortunate bullying experience in elementary school can cause you to opt out of traditional schooling methods for your child and homeschool instead. Although these situations may not cause significant changes in your parenting "style" per say, they may alter the experiences you allow your child to have.

Your Self-Esteem/Self-Image

Self-esteem can be defined as the way you see yourself, whether positive or negative. It is sometimes referred as *self-image* or *self-worth* (Santrock 97). When you have a high self-esteem, you have a positive view of who you are and what it is you do. Folks with a positive self-image are confident, secure in their sense of identity, and are able to tolerate and manage confrontation in appropriate ways. Individuals with a low self-esteem have much self-doubt. They need the approval of others to help them feel good about the person they are, and struggle with confrontation due to their insecurities.

So, let's begin to understand how self-esteem affects your parenting. A parent who has a high self-esteem is less likely to struggle with parenting. In fact, individuals with a high self-esteem are more likely to have appropriate attachment with their children, as well as utilize more authoritative parenting styles.

Because they are confident in who they are, they have less of a need to seek approval or gain favor from their children, their co-parent, and/or others. They are less likely to want to be the "cool" mom or be their child's "friend."

As you can imagine, if you have a low self-esteem you may be more likely to engage in Permissive parenting styles, but for the wrong reasons. Instead of being a Permissive parent because you want too and you value your child's own opinion and identity, you engage in Permissive parenting because you are afraid to deal with confrontation. Parents who have low self-esteem are more likely to give in to their children because there is a subconscious need to have their approval. You need to feel as though you are well-loved and well-liked. As such, you give in to your children, becoming the Weak Zebra.

A poor self-esteem can also affect your parenting in the way that you interact with your co-parent. It is not uncommon for parents to have differing parenting styles. At times, you might find a couple who agree approximately 80% of the time on how to parent their children, but seldom more than that. If you have a high self-esteem, you are less likely to struggle with issues such as challenging your co-parent on how *they* want to parent versus how *you* want to parent. You and your co-parent are more likely to discuss parenting choices and hot topics, such as discipline, in an appropriate way. Parents who have a low self-esteem will either not confront their co-parent on the issue at hand or will engage with them in an aggressive and inappropriate way.

I think we all know a couple who has differing parenting styles and are frequently arguing with one another in front of everyone. They may be at a restaurant, at a party, or at the house of an in-law; they still argue. Furthermore, their arguments are not typically very graceful in any way. As a bystander, it can be very uncomfortable to watch, and is very disturbing for the children of this couple. Can you think of someone who matches this description? If you can, I bet you can also identify that at least one, or both, partners have a poor self-esteem.

Your Emotional & Mental Health

In the workplace, it is common knowledge that happy employees are better and more productive. In the parenting world, it is no different. A happy mommy is a better mommy. A father who feels fulfilled in his life, is a better daddy. Being in a happy and emotionally healthy state of mind is key to, not only being the best parent that you can be, but to achieving your vision of the perfect parent. One of the most significant barriers to joyful parenting can be mental health issues, such as depression, anxiety, and trauma reactions. Any mental health condition can impact how successfully you administer discipline, engage with your children, communicate with your co-parent, and accomplish daily household tasks.

Research has shown that conditions, such as postpartum depression, can significantly impact healthy attachment creation between a mother and her infant. As such, the children of women who suffer from postpartum depression have a higher likelihood of developing poor attachment styles, having emotional conditions, and displaying inappropriate behaviors in early childhood. For example, a mother who has postpartum depression will have less energy, experiencing more fatigue and less motivation. She will find no pleasure in activities that she may have once found enjoyable. As such, when the child attempts to interact with her by bringing her a rattle found on the floor, the mother is less likely to interact with the child, ignoring him. This sends the message to the child that his emotional needs are not important to his mother, and thus are not important at all. The same child may have a dirty diaper, and due to the lethargy that can be experienced with postpartum depression, the mother may take more time to address this simple need. As such, the child may begin to cry to signal to his mother that he needs something. Due to her postpartum depression, however, she will be more forgetful and less patient. As such, she may forget to check his diaper, and will become more irritable and annoyed by his incessant crying. This, in turn, may cause for the child's diaper to go unchanged for a length of time, which then signals to the child that his physical needs are not important to her, and as such, are not important at all. This is how poor attachment is formed between an infant and a mother who may not be in an emotionally healthy state of mind.

Even if a mother or father does not have a mental health condition, a parent can still be in a negative state of mind due to simple conditions that we all experience, such as stress. Stress can come from anywhere: work, home, in-laws, your family, or even your own children can cause you to feel large amounts of stress which, in turn, will affect how you parent. When you are stressed, you are more irritable, less patient, and more likely to be harsh in discipline. During times of stress or exhaustion, you are also more likely to give in to your child when they tantrum or argue with you. This, in turn, makes you less consistent as parent, and more likely to engage in, what I like to call, "couch parenting" (i.e. a parent who is giving minimal effort in parenting their child and may, literally, be sitting on a sofa, shouting directives to their child, but never actually moving from their position).

In our society today, there is a large taboo when it comes to mental health conditions. Many people suffer from a mental health disorder, but never seek help for it. This is unnecessary. There is no reason to suffer from a mental health condition when there is ample and effective help available. If you suspect that you may be suffering from a mental health disorder, please seek out help from a mental health professional, such as a marriage and family therapist.

Your Personality

Personality is a fascinating subject, and as a therapist, has been one of the most interesting things to study. Paplia and Feldman defined personality as a mixture of emotions, thoughts, temperament, and behaviors that remain consistent over time. This mixture is what makes each person unique in who they are and how they interact with the world (204). Psychologists have worked hard to understand the dimensions that form personality, and many researchers believe that they have accomplished this, defining 5 factors that they believe are the core of personality. These factors are openness, conscientiousness, extraversion, agreeableness, and emotional stability. These 5 dimensions are known as the **Big Five Factors of Personality**.

As you can imagine, not all psychologists agree with the Big Five. Some believe that there are other factors that should be included, such as positivity and self-assertiveness. Regardless, a number of research studies suggest that the Big Five are important components to think of when discussing personality (Santrock 135).

For our purposes, it's important to know that personality is largely created by your genetic makeup, life experiences, and your attachment style. Your personality governs everything that you do with regard to how you interact and engage with the world. As such, your personality governs how you manage your own emotions, how you manage conflict, and how you communicate with the people around you, among other things. As such, it is easy to see how your personality would greatly affect your parenting.

Your Co-Parent

A co-parent is the person with whom you are sharing the parenting responsibilities of your children. Traditionally, co-parents are the biological mom and dad of the child, but in today's modern age, they may consist of stepparents, adoptive parents, grandparents, foster parents, daycare workers, etc. Every family is different in terms of who is sharing the responsibility to parent the children. It can be agreed, however, that your co-parent is going to affect the way that you parent. For example, if you have a co-parent who is very lenient in their parenting, letting your child get away with everything, you are more likely to try and overcompensate by being firmer and stricter with your child. The reverse may also be true, where if your co-parent is very strict, you may find yourself allowing your child to slide on certain rules in an effort to soften the parenting environment in the home.

In some situations, you may have a co-parent who doesn't parent at all. Your children can be running amok in your home and your co-parent will do nothing. This can be incredibly frustrating for you, causing more conflict and tension between you and your co-parent. You may also find yourself in a situation where your co-parent lacks respect for you and your opinions of how a specific parenting task should be managed. In fact, this co-parent may be undermining your own parenting. As such, this indirectly affects the way you parent.

Given all of these different examples, it is easy to see how your co-parent can either play a positive or negative role in how you manage your children. It is important that co-parents share a similar parenting vision, agreeing on how most parenting tasks will be managed in and out of the home. This topic is so important that, later in this text, we will discuss in much more detail how to align your parenting vision with that of your co-parent.

Your Parenting Style & Your Child: The Goodness of Fit

Goodness of Fit is a concept that has to do with how appropriate an environment matches a child. Essentially, does the child and his personality match the demands of his or her environment, or does the parent (and who that parent is) match up well with the child, and who that child is. It should be noted that a child and a parent do not need to be a perfect match. The better the match, however, the more likely that the parent and the child will have a strong, healthy, and positive Parent-Child relationship. Alicia Lieberman explains that Goodness of Fit is when a child's capacity and motivation is matched with the expectations and demands of the parent. A poor fit exists when a child lacks the ability to fulfill the expectations of the parent (102-103).

In order to better understand this concept, consider the following analogy. Pretend that you are out shopping for a pair of shoes. You try on various sizes until you find the shoe and size that fits best. It may not be perfect, but it fits well, it fits comfortably, and you like the shoe you have chosen. This is a good fit. Now, let's say that you went shopping for a pair of shoes and found a pair that you liked, but could not find your size. Depending on how much you really like the shoe, you may opt to try a half size larger or half a size smaller. In this situation, the shoe may still fit well, but it may not be as comfortable. This is not a good fit, but it is a match that will work and still get you where you need to go. Now, let's look at one more example. Let's say when you are shopping for that shoe that you love so much, you can't find your size, nor can you find a half size smaller or larger. Your only option is to buy a shoe that is a full size smaller or larger. When you put on the smaller size, the shoe causes blisters and your toes are curled up at the front. When you put on the larger size, the shoes fall right off as you walk. In this situation, you need a pair of shoes, you really like this pair, but the fit doesn't work at all. It's a poor fit.

Similar to these shoes, this is what goodness-of-fit is all about. Either you and your child go together perfectly like that first pair of shoes, or you go together well enough, like the second pair of shoes, or you don't go together at all like the last pair. Even with that last pair of shoes, you still love the shoes, they just don't fit. Similarly, you still love your child, you just don't fit well together.

Who you are as a person (i.e. your personality, your parenting style, your attachment style) will either line up with who your child is or it won't. Your child's temperament and personality may be at complete odds with who you are as a parent, and as such, parenting this child will be much more challenging for you. On the other hand, if who you are as a person lines up with who your child is, then you will find that your ability to parent this child seems to come naturally because the fit between you and your child is a good match.

The question now may be, what do you do if you and your child are not a good fit for one another? The answer to this is not easy. In most cases, it will require you, as the parent, to change how you parent this child in order to match them more appropriately. This, however, is not an easy task because it will require you to go against your natural parenting default. It can be done successfully, however, and we will discuss this in more depth later on in this text.

4.3 The Next Steps....

Over the course of these last few chapters, we have been building a thorough understanding of who *you* are as a parent, as well as the different components that are coming together to create your current parenting-self. Hopefully, you have come to see parenting is like a giant, intricately designed spider web, where everything is connected to everything else, and changing or altering one part of the web will most certainly affect the rest of it. Parenting is far from being one dimensional! You must have a firm understanding of how all of these pieces come together to create the picture that is you and your current family system. In doing this, you'll be better able to see where the "hiccups" are, and thus, better able to formulate and implement change.

At this point, our foundation is set. We can now begin to look at the different ways you can begin to improve your Parent-Child relationship, correct problematic behaviors (such as anger outbursts), solve parenting issues with your co-parent, and tackle parental burn-out.

5

Your Parent-Child Relationship & How to Improve It

5.1 The Power of Human Connection

To begin this section, I want to tell you a story about a child. This is a true story about myself, in all honesty, about when I was in high school. I can truthfully say my father and I had a very positive, strong, and wonderful Parent-Child relationship. It is a relationship that has always thrived, and continues to thrive, to this very day. This isn't a long story, but I think that the story I'm going to tell you will help you to understand why a Parent-Child relationship built upon love and trust is so useful to you as you raise your child now, and in the future.

Now, I think we can all remember our high school days. Today, I work with many teenagers, all of whom have been offered drugs in some way, shape, or form while at school. This, of course, is something no parent wants to hear, but it is the truth nonetheless. When I was in high school, it was no different. I remember it was my freshman year, and I was sitting in my English class. I had been assigned a desk towards the back of the classroom beside a girl who was known to use drugs. It was only a matter of time before she would come to offer me some. It didn't take long for me to answer her. As my options fluttered in my head, one thing stood out very clearly to me: If I were to get caught, my dad would have been devastated and disappointed. As this fact became clearer to me, I decided to tell this girl "no." It is important to point out that I did not say "no" because I was afraid of getting caught. I said "no," because I was afraid of disappointing my dad. *That* is the power of the Parent-Child relationship.

A strong Parent-Child relationship offers many benefits to you and your child. Research has shown that a positive relationship can increase communication between you and your child, decrease hostility and aggression in children, and improve their social skills. It can decrease the possibility of drug use by teens, decrease problematic behaviors, and potentially increase self-esteem. Furthermore, as if these benefits weren't enough, a strong, positive Parent-Child relationship offers a protective factor against mental health conditions such as depression and anxiety, as well as serious risk behaviors such as suicide and non-suicidal self-harm (such as cutting). To help demonstrate this, I want to share with you another story about a real client who I worked with. This story is about a 17-year-old male by the name of Eric No, this story doesn't necessarily demonstrate the power of the Parent-Child relationship, but it does demonstrate the power of human connection, which is the root of the Parent-Child relationship.

Eric was a client of mine some years ago, and he had been assigned to me randomly by my Clinic Supervisor. I was known for my work with teens who engaged in non-suicidal self-harm and depression. Eric had been diagnosed with a depressive disorder and had a long history of trying to commit suicide and of cutting behaviors. When I met Eric, I instantly was struck by how charming and sweet he was. He was very respectful in sessions with me, and he was always willing to discuss his problems. I had been seeing Eric for approximately 2 months, which is not that long considering that sessions were one time a week for an hour. Eric had been doing well, with no suicidal ideations, and had made some significant improvements in reducing his cutting behavior. Early on in our relationship, Eric was asking me several questions about my qualifications as a therapist. This can be fairly common in therapy since many clients want to make sure that you are the right person for them and their problems. He had asked me if I had ever lost anyone to suicide, to which I replied "no." Fast forward to two months later where Eric and I are sitting in a session together. It was a Monday, and I remember asking him how his weekend had gone. He said to me that it went, "Kind of bad." When I asked him to clarify, he explained the following:

> "Over the weekend I became really depressed. Nothing I did seemed to cheer me up, and I started to think a lot about suicide. I didn't just think about it a lot, I actually planned

it out. I decided I was going to hang myself in my parents' garage. I was going to use my belt, and I was going to wait until after my parents left for the day to go run errands. I knew they would be gone for at least 2 hours, and this was plenty of time for me to kill myself. When they left, I took the belt, went to the garage, and prepped everything. I had already written a note to my parents explaining why I was killing myself and telling them that I was sorry. I looped the belt over one of the rafters in the garage and stood up on this tall stool. I looped the belt around my neck, closed my eyes, and got ready to jump."

As you can imagine, I was completely entranced by the story, but also confused. Why was Eric not in a hospital? So, I asked him, what happened.

"Obviously you are not dead because you are sitting right here in front of me. I'm also going to guess that you weren't found hanging unconscious in the garage because, if you were, I would think you would be in the hospital right now. So, what happened? Did your parents walk in on you?"

Eric replied, "No, I never jumped."

"Why not? What happened? What kept you from jumping?"

He replied, "You. When I was standing there with the belt around my neck, I remembered that you told me you had never lost anyone to suicide before. And at that moment, I decided, I didn't want to be your first."

My relationship with Eric, the human connection I had developed with him, was so strong, so powerful, and so positive in his life, that it saved him. As you can imagine, I cried in that therapy room with Eric that day, and I am not ashamed to share that. This story should further show you how a positive relationship with your child can make all the difference in the choices that they make that could affect their future permanently. The power of human connection is one of the strongest and most effective tools I have as a therapist, and it's one of the most important tools you have as a parent. It's necessary to note that connection with your child is a life-long process. Once you've built it up, you need to nurture it consistently over time. The work is never truly done.

So, now that we have an understanding about how important this relationship truly is, the time has come to begin discussing how we create it, on a continuous basis, throughout the lifespan of your child.

5.2 How to Create a Strong, Positive Relationship with Your Child

What I would like to teach you is what I like to call the "Emotional Piggy Bank." At this point, we already know how to create a healthy attachment with infants, but as children grow older, the Parent-Child relationship can become more difficult to manage and nurture. That is what this chapter is all about. To begin, let's discuss what the Emotional Piggy Bank is.

The Emotional Piggy Bank

The **Emotional Piggy Bank** is how relationships work. Imagine a bank account, except that this is an *emotional* bank account. Every relationship you have has its own separate account that you share with them (i.e. one account for you and your spouse, a second account for you and your child, a third account for your spouse and your child). Every time you engage with a person in a positive way, you are depositing funds into your emotional bank account with that particular person. Every time you engage in an argument or do something that offends or hurts the other person, you are withdrawing funds from that emotional bank account. The more funds you deposit, the wealthier your account becomes. The more funds you withdraw from the account, the poorer your account becomes. As with your real bank accounts, your goal should always be to be in the black, with sufficient funds in your account to live comfortably. No one likes to be in debt, and so the same principle is true of the Emotional Piggy Bank.

Building a positive Parent-Child relationship, is all about continuously depositing funds into the Emotional Piggy Bank that you share with your child. Every time you reprimand them, discipline them, yell at them, etc., you are withdrawing funds from that account. Every time you engage with them in a way that is nourishing and positive, you deposit funds into the account. Depending on your child's age, how you nurse the relationship will be different. If you have an infant, feeding them, singing to them, rocking them, and so on, are all ways you would deposit funds. If you have a toddler, playing peek-a-boo with them, or swinging them at a park, are ways that you may engage with them to deposit funds. If you have a teenager, going out together for a bite to eat, or seeing a movie together, cooking together, working on a car together, supporting them at their baseball games, and so forth, are all ways that you may be able to deposit funds into your emotional bank account. Essentially, the more quality time you have with your child, the richer that account becomes. The richer your account becomes, the more the account can withstand hardship. So, if your teen decides to lie to you, and you and your teen have a huge, blowout argument, you will be making a huge withdrawal from the account. But, because the account was so rich to begin with, it can withstand this large withdrawal and, as such, does not go into the red. These are the basics for developing a positive Parent-Child relationship.

Now that we know the basics, let's talk about all the different ways that you can contribute to your Emotional Piggy Bank with your child.

Creating a "Rich" Emotional Bank Account

There are many ways to create a "rich" emotional bank account. I'll spend some time and discuss 3 of them, elaborating and helping you to really understand how these items come together to make for a positive Parent-Child relationship. In this section, the 3 items we will be looking at are:

- Quality Time
- Family Narrative

- Admitting Parental Failure

Quality Time

As I have already hinted, one of the best ways to begin building a rich emotional bank account with your child is by spending lots of quality time with them. I define **Quality time** as spending time engaging in an activity that the other person enjoys. That means that, in order for your activity to "count" as quality time, and thus, "deposit" funds into that account, it must be something your child enjoys too! There are tons of ways to engage in quality time, you just need to get creative and make this a priority!

As a therapist, I have frequently prescribed family time as homework for families. This homework is sometimes referred to as "attending" in the mental health community. I have found that having dedicated time each day for the family to spend together in an enjoyable activity did wonders for helping to decrease anger outbursts and defiant behaviors. Part of what having regular family time does is create a positive family narrative and culture. Regular time spent together helps to create and improve the parent-child relationship. This is done by creating positive interactions between siblings and caregivers.

If you find that you might be guilty of not spending enough time with your children, I recommend that you try the following practice. Aim to set aside at least 10 minutes every day to spend with each one of your children, engaging in an activity of *their* choice. During your interactions with your child, try to show a sincere interest in the activities they have chosen. Be sure to turn off the TV or put away tablets, cell phones, and computers and truly give your child your undivided attention for at least 10 minutes. During this time, show a sincere interest in what they're doing by providing enthusiastic commentary or positive statements about the activity they are engaging in. For example, if your child has decided to color with you, perhaps praise their use of color, or comment on how well they have drawn a tree or a person. Allow your child the opportunity to lead the activity and try to refrain from making suggestions, asking questions, and/or criticizing your child.

During this activity, you may notice that your child engages in negative behaviors because your child may not be familiar with this kind of interaction from you. If this happens, try the following:

- Ignore the negative behavior by looking away or simply not responding to it.
- Refrain from scolding or lecturing your child. Doing this may backfire by providing attention for misbehavior. This, inadvertently, rewards the negative behavior.
- If your child continues being disruptive (or dangerous) during the one-on-one time, stop the one-on-one time for that day. By doing this, you are sending the opposite message to your child, that engaging in negative behavior results in no attention from you.

Overtime, as you consistently spend these 10 minutes a day with your child, you will see a decrease in negative behaviors and an increase in positive behaviors from your child as they begin to see that engaging in "good" behavior gets attention from you and "negative" behavior results in no attention.

For busy parents, it's hard to find those 10 minutes a day for every child. There are many ways you can creatively spend positive time with your child, however, while also taking care of your daily tasks. If this is an area you struggle with, consider checking out my other book, *Trials of the Working Parent*, where I go into much more detail on how to increase quality time with your children while also managing daily life. You can also visit my website (kcdreisbach.com) where I have several blog posts tackling this topic. I also have a Pinterest Resource page (pinterest.com/kcdreisbach), where I pin tons of ideas from parents all over the world that can help you manage this in your daily life.

Family Narrative

A family narrative can be a complex concept to explain. Essentially, a **family narrative** is the story of your family, as told by any given person in your family. It is the perspective of that particular person. For example, when I think of my family, I recall hundreds of positive stories. Occasionally, I might think of a sad event, such as a death, or of an argument that was particularly rough, but, overall, the memories are bright and happy. Furthermore, when I imagine the different members in my family, positive descriptions come to mind because I see them all as wonderful people. Since the stories I remember and the adjectives I would use to describe my family members are all strongly positive, then I most likely have a positive family narrative. If, when I tell the story of my family, I talk about how angry my dad always was, how much my brother and sister fought all the time, and how I spent most of my time alone in my room, etc., then my family narrative is more bleak and more negative. The goal is for you to develop, and help your child develop, a positive and happy family narrative.

I'm going to take some time to explain why this is important. In depression there is a theory on how to treat depression by using something called "behavioral activation." The theory is that when people become depressed, they begin to isolate, and they start to view the world in a negative way because they are sad. The more they isolate, the less they do the things that they once used to enjoy. The less they do the things that they once used to enjoy, the fewer memories they have of joyful things. The more time they spend alone and sad, the more memories they have of being alone and sad. What ends up happening is that the narrative of their life becomes a story about depression; a story about being depressed and alone. This, in turn, feeds back into the depression causing a vicious cycle that makes the person spiral further and further down into that depressed state.

With **behavioral activation**, the therapist assigns the client activities to do that are supposed to help increase positive memories for the client. Activities might be to go for a walk with a friend, to call a friend and talk to them about a movie, to go out to dinner with a spouse, and so on. The principle behind behavioral activation is that, as the client engages in more and more activities that he enjoys and likes, he begins to form more memories that are positive. The more positive memories he forms, the less his story becomes about depression (Selva, *Be-*

havioural Activation). The less his story becomes about depression, the more joy he is going to feel, and the less depressed he will become. This, in turn, causes the client to begin reversing that spiral, spiraling up and out of depression.

When we talk about positive family narratives, we are essentially using the same idea behind behavioral activation. By creating and engaging in various activities that are positive to the people involved, we are helping the child and the parent to develop positive memories which, in turn, creates a positive family narrative. This means that we are depositing lots of funds into the emotional bank account.

Admitting Parental Failure

As human beings, we all make mistakes, but being able to admit we're wrong is huge. I think we have all had the experience where a friend, or someone you know, made a mistake but refused to admit it. This, most likely, made you angry, annoyed, frustrated, and very hurt. Furthermore, I have known people who have actually broken up and ended their relationship with someone because one of them refused to admit that they were wrong. Making mistakes as a parent can withdraw funds from that emotional bank account, but you can help replace those funds by admitting you've made a mistake. This can be very hard to do.

For most folks, it is really hard to admit you're wrong or to admit that you have made a mistake. Pride often gets in the way of this. Being able to admit that you made a mistake to your child can not only assist in depositing depleted funds from your

Emotional Piggy Bank, but it can also assist in healing and repairing a damaged Parent-Child relationship. Furthermore, it actually models to your child how to take responsibility for one's actions. Moreover, if you, as a parent, can go a step further and ask for forgiveness from your child, you will model to them a lesson in humility.

Even as a therapist, I have made many mistakes as a parent and, when I have made mistakes, I do my very best to admit them to my child. There was a time that I was very stressed from work and struggling to get a lot of chores done at home. My daughter, five-years-old at the time, was desperate for my attention. She kept coming to me saying, "Mommy, look at this," or, "Look at that," and so on. I became really frustrated and I snapped at her. Her eyes became wide with shock and then instantly drooped down in sadness. Her lips slowly turned from a smile to a frown, and I could see that I had hurt my poor little girl's feelings, who was just so excited to share with me all of the wonders that she had discovered. She felt dejected and unwanted at that moment. And I felt terrible. I took a deep breath, and I realized that I had made a mistake; that I had allowed my own stress from work to seep into how I was treating and interacting with her. I made a mistake. I took another deep breath, took her hand in my own, and knelt down on one knee. I looked up at her and I said softly, "I am so sorry. I shouldn't have snapped at you. I should have used my words, and calmly told you to wait a few minutes until Mommy could take care of something. I shouldn't have yelled. Will you forgive me?" Of course my daughter forgave me, saying something to the effect of, "It's okay Mommy. Just remember, next time, I'll have to give you a Time Out."

Asking our children for forgiveness, and admitting when we have made a mistake, can be an invaluable teaching tool. Just like we discussed earlier in this book, the way you interact with your child serves as a model to your child about how he or she should interact with the world. That is why it is so important for us to model to our children the behaviors we want to see in them. If you want a child who is compassionate, then you must show them compassion. If you want a child who values forgiveness, then you must ask and give forgiveness. If you want a child who uses their words in a calm manner when upset, then you must use your words in a calm manner when you are upset.

Another important note to make is that you must give your child the opportunity to share his own emotions when you are admitting parental failure. If you go to your child, tell them you made a mistake and are asking for forgiveness, you must be prepared for your child to tell you that they do not forgive you, or that they're hurt by what you have done. These are not easy things to hear, nor are they pleasant to deal with. You must be able to tolerate them. This is extremely important. In life, we all have to deal with news that is not pleasant, and in tolerating this type of news from your child, you are, once again, modeling to them how to accept the negative in a gracious way.

Finally, when it comes to admitting parental failure, you should do this no matter how old your child is. Whether you are holding an infant in your arms or they're 18-years-old, when you make a mistake, admit it, and ask for forgiveness. It's common for parents to forget that their infant deserves to hear these words too. A parent may recognize that what they did or said to the baby was wrong but then fail to take that extra step to apologize. It might seem silly, but this is important for a variety of reasons:

1. Your infant is listening. They may not fully understand you yet, but they can interpret facial expressions and your tone of voice. These things help to carry your message to them, even if they can't understand your words.
2. Beginning this practice when your child is an infant helps to stretch and exercise these "parenting muscles." For some of us, this practice is going to be really hard to do. So, start practicing early on before your child has the ability to verbally respond to your request for forgiveness. The more you practice, the easier it will get.
3. Remember principle 7 from my parenting philosophy (i.e. *The core of the Parent-Child relationship must be in respect.*)? Here's one way that principle is being reflected. By apologizing and asking for forgiveness, you are showing your infant from the very beginning that they are deserving and worthy of respect.

As rich as your Emotional Piggy Bank may be, there is always a possibility that it becomes damaged over time. Just like any relationship, as humans, we make mistakes that can affect the relationship, and sometimes, those mistakes may be way too big, causing a rich account to become entirely depleted in one big swoop! In our next section, I'm going to discuss a little bit about the different ways the Parent-Child relationship can become damaged.

5.3 Damaging the Parent-Child Relationship & How to Repair It

Most simply, a damaged Parent-Child relationship is one in which there is an overdraft of funds pulled from the Emotional Piggy Bank. The most obvious causes to a damaged relationship are forms of child abuse, such as sexual abuse, physical abuse, neglect, and emotional/psychological abuse. Engaging in activities that can be considered abusive are highly damaging to the Parent-Child relationship and have a high likelihood of causing mental health issues and behavioral problems in children. If you suspect that you or someone you know might be engaging in abusive behaviors, please consider consulting with a family therapist to discuss how to address these issues in your home.

Another way that the Parent-Child relationship can become damaged (i.e. an overdraft of the emotional bank account) is when you have a parent who's emotional well-being has been impacted negatively in some way. I'm sure you have heard of the title "Angry Mommy," which usually references a parent who is seemingly angry *all* the time. It's typically a mother or father who is highly stressed, overwhelmed, and in need of a big break!

Apart from being stressed, mental health issues can also cause parents to be emotionally unavailable to the child. This can be due to past trauma (for the parent), or insecurities leading to low self-esteem, compromising the parent's ability to manage or handle the child's emotions. These items can also lead to a parent failing to create a positive family narrative. The good news is that the damage caused to a Parent-Child relationship can always be repaired!

As mentioned previously, the key to a strong Parent-Child relationship is a strong and positive family narrative. Building memories with your child and responding to your child's needs are one of the important ways of repairing the damaged relationship.

Now that you know all about the Emotional Piggy Bank, you need to take the time to evaluate how your account currently looks. Are you in the positive? Are you in the negative? Is it neutral? No matter where your account is at, you can always repair it and/or improve it by creating positive family memories. This will help in building a positive family narrative. If you remember earlier in this chapter, we discussed Behavioral Activation, and how it brings people back from depression. Similar to behavioral activation, your family narrative is the way that you can bring your relationship back into a positive state. Always remember that the family narrative is the key to a happy family.

6

Understanding Psychosocial Development in Children

I am a big believer of the old adage, "Knowledge is Power." I think this is particularly true when we talk about understanding our children and why they behave the way that they do. Frequently, comprehending the root cause (or the "why") of behavior helps parents to better identify what they can do to help support positive changes in their child. As such, this chapter is designed to help you understand your child's psychological, social, and emotional development from infancy to early adulthood. Santrock defined **development** as "the pattern of biological, cognitive, and socioemotional processes that begins at conception and continues through the life span" (28).

In order to make this chapter more manageable, it will be broken down into a few sections: infancy (0 to 3 years of age), early childhood (approximately 3 years to 6 years of age), middle childhood (from about 6 to 11 years of age), and adolescence (from about 12 to 20 years of age). It is important to note that there are many different theorists that have developed models about how human beings grow. As a parent, you don't need to worry about the multitude of theories out there or who devised them. All you need to have is a basic understanding of what your child is going through at different developmental stages. That's what I'm hoping to provide you in this chapter. This information should give you a rough sketch of what is going on in your child's mind while also providing you with some foundational knowledge we can use as we discuss behaviors and behavioral change in later chapters.

6.1 Development in Infancy

During the first three years of life, the psychosocial and physical development of children is fast and significant. In just three short years, children go from immobile entities who are 100% dependent on their caregivers, to unique individuals who have their own needs, wants, and plans. This age group also presents one of the more challenging times in the Parent-Child relationship... the Terrible Twos! Since development during these years are so impactful, it's a good idea to further break down this age range, looking at each year of life to better understand what is going on in our children's hearts and minds.

Birth to 12 Months

From the very beginning, children have their own personalities. Although there are many common behaviors that are similar in infants, such as basic sucking reflexes, babies still show signs of their own, unique personality as early as the first few days of life. If you are a parent of multiple kids, you can vouch for this statement! Some infants are "easy babies," eat lazily, or spend most days sleeping. Others might be described as "difficult babies" or colicky, requiring constant rocking in order to soothe them. My own children were (and still are) at opposite ends of the personality spectrum. Still, despite these differences, all children will master different social skills and develop cognitively and psychologically in similar ways.

From birth to approximately 6 months of age, infants display interest in the world around them, and have a desire to engage socially with the significant people in their lives. They begin to smile, babble, and coo at their parents, yearning for interaction with them. Language is still far from being mastered, but some children may say a few, simple words at this time. They are working hard to gain mobility by crawling or scooting and are also developing other large motor skills. Finally, trust begins to form as the baby's needs are met (or not met) by the caregiver, setting the stage for the Parent-Child relationship and attachment with the parent.

From 6 months of age to 1 year, a full range of emotions become visible and are communicated more clearly through behavior. As parents, we are able to tell if our child is sad, scared, angry, or surprised. The child still has few words that he can use to express himself, but other ways of communicating erupt at this time, such as clapping, belly laughs, and the shaking of the head to indicate "no" or "yes." During this time, children continue to try and engage with the people around them and are mostly focused on their primary caregiver. A fear of strangers may develop at this time, causing the baby to cling to his parents in new or unfamiliar situations. Lastly, attachment relationships are solidified during this time.

1 Year to 2 Years

Although physical development of children during this age range is not nearly as impressive as birth to 12 months, psychosocial development is fantastic! Language development at this time is also amazing, with children going from just a few simple words, to a large vocabulary. Some little ones will speak in short phrases, stringing words together to help their caregivers understand their wants and needs. The ability to walk and run are mastered, as well as climbing (on everything!), throwing, and even jumping can be seen during this time. The desire to explore the world is evident, but emotionally, our little ones still need us, their parents, to hold and cuddle them when the world becomes too overwhelming. Fearfulness of new people and situations continues to rise and peak during this time period. The early stages of empathy begin to develop, and the attachment the child has developed with his parents will now begin to affect the relationship he has with others. Finally, towards the end of this time period, children will begin to show the beginnings of temper tantrums, which are loathed and feared by ALL parents!

2 Years to 3 Years

As our young ones come into the second half of toddlerhood, emotions continue to develop as toddlers in this age group begin to evaluate themselves. Emotions such as empathy, embarrassment, and jealousy fully emerge, with the beginnings of guilt and shame taking root. We continue to see the fear of new situations and people throughout this time, and temper tantrums occur regularly as our toddlers begin to assert their will and become frustrated when they can't. Finally, language continues to explode with new word acquisitions occurring almost daily. They continue to string words together to form phrases, making it easier to understand their needs and wants. Some kids might even begin to speak in full sentences during this time.

6.2 Development in Early Childhood

Early childhood is a remarkable time. Your child's ability to communicate with you using words and appropriate body language fully comes into play by the end of early childhood. The Terrible Twos are gone, and there is peace in the home as your child becomes much easier to manage. The preschool years come and go, and the elementary school years step in. Your child becomes increasingly social with others, makes friends, and his personality is in full bloom, revealing to you a clear image of the person your child will become.

During early childhood, your child will make huge advances in understanding himself, as well as developing a deeper understanding of his emotions. With this understanding comes the ability to self-regulate, which is an important step towards controlling and managing difficult emotions, such as anger. Helping your child to understand their feelings during early childhood is an important step. Without teaching your child emotion regulation, you risk temper tantrums and anger outbursts as a common and regular occurrence in your household. Language fully develops during this time, with your child's speech being akin to that of an adult. Finally, your child's pattern of social interaction becomes more habitual, and as such, patterns of bullying behavior or victimization may become established at this time.

6.3 Development in Middle Childhood

In middle childhood, children become physically capable of anything! With improved balance, increased speed, and more control, children are highly active during this time. Running, jumping, climbing, and skipping, among other large motor skills, are fully developed. It's important to keep kids moving during this time, ensuring that they get plenty of physical exercise for overall health and well-being. Cognitively, children in middle childhood understand cause and effect, have the ability to consider multiple perspectives at one time, and multitasking becomes much easier to manage.

Emotion regulation is greatly improved during middle childhood, especially if caregivers have helped their child develop a good understanding of emotion and healthy coping skills to manage difficult feelings. The foundation built early on in the Parent-Child relationship helps to create harmony and mutual understanding between the child and the parent, setting the stage for the challenging years ahead in adolescence. Finally, towards the end of middle childhood, friendships become more intimate, and the opinions of friends begin to outweigh the opinions of caregivers.

6.4 Development in Adolescence

Adolescence is a trying time for parents. Puberty hits and, with it, a wave of physical and emotional changes. Sexuality develops with an increasing curiosity and desire to explore the opposite (or same) sex as the body becomes sexually mature for procreation (something no parent really wants to deal with). With puberty comes the wave of cliché mood swings that can leave parents feeling confused and exhausted. During this time, children are trying to discover who they are in comparison to their parents and their peers, and they are trying to determine where they belong in society. It's an awkward time.... As our teens try to discover their own personal identity, they also clash frequently with us, butting heads with their parents on an almost daily basis. This consistent bickering and "attitude-giving" is a sign of **individuation**, the natural process of gaining a sense of individuality (i.e. forming a separate identity from others, such as parents) (Amsel, *Individuation*). It is a normal struggle in gaining autonomy for teens and young adults, but a total headache for us as parents!

In many ways, adolescence mirrors toddlerhood where, in both cases, the child is caught between wanting to be free to do as he wishes but is also not quite ready to face the world alone. There is a teeter-tottering that occurs as the child struggles between wanting independence and needing parental support. Adolescence comes complete with temper tantrums too! Just replace throwing themselves on the floor with door slamming and stomping out of the room.

* * *

Although this chapter is not extensive in any way, this brief rundown of child psychosocial development should be enough of a foundation for us to work off of as we discuss the Parent-Child relationship from birth to adulthood. If you want to know more about your child's development, I recommend checking out the following books and websites for additional reading to supplement this chapter.

- *The Emotional Life of the Toddler* by Alicia F. Lieberman
- *Ages and Stages: A Parent's Guide to Normal Childhood Development* by Charles Schaefer and Theresa Foy DiGeronimo
- *Erik Erikson's Stages of Psychosocial Development* by Saul McLeod (simplypsychology.org)

- *Physical and Psychosocial Development Resources for Parents of Adolescents and Young Adults* by the Society for Adolescent Health and Medicine (adolescenthealth.org)
- *Signs of Normal Development Stages* by The Whole Child (thewholechild.org)

7

Understanding Emotions & Behavior in Children

Emotions are complex. They are a normal part of being human, and to be devoid of emotions is problematic. In many ways, however, emotions are beautiful. Imagine trying to live your life without feeling joy or love? Life would be pretty boring, but I think we could all do without fear, anger, or sadness, right? Wrong! Those emotions play a vital role in our safety, survival, and even help us in task accomplishment. Emotions are vital to human behavior and understanding the role emotions play in behavior is key to knowing how to manage difficult emotions in children.

There is a popular therapy that has been used for years, known as *Cognitive Behavioral Therapy* (CBT). There are many layers to this therapeutic approach, but there is one particular point that we will discuss here as we learn more about emotions and behaviors in children. In CBT, a therapist works with an individual by changing his or her thought process in order to change behavior. The theory is based on the idea that the mind is continuously thinking and producing thoughts. Essentially, we all have a non-stop, internal dialogue going on in our own minds. These thoughts produce emotions, which, in turn, produce behavior.

Thought ⟶ Emotion/Feeling ⟶ Behavior/Action

To help you understand how this concept plays out in everyday scenarios, let's look at an example. Let's say your boss asks to meet with you. Your first thought might be, *"Oh no, I'm in trouble."* This thought will elicit an emotion, most likely anxiety, which will produce a behavioral response (i.e. you might double check that your work was done and completed correctly). On the contrary, if your first thought is something more like, *"Yes! I'm finally getting promoted,"* the triggered emotional response will be excitement or joy, and the triggered behavior may be calling your spouse to tell them about your possible promotion. This is a fairly simplified explanation of this concept, but it is the general idea.

Understanding how thoughts relate to emotions, which then triggers behaviors, lays the foundation for understanding our children's behaviors. From there, we need to understand what types of behaviors are elicited by different emotions. If I ask you to name emotions, you will probably think of several: fear, anxiety, anger, jealousy, joy, love, etc. For the purposes of this chapter, I am going to boil emotions down to a basic few: joy, anger, fear, anxiety, and sadness. I think it could be argued that most emotions stem from these five. For example, jealousy, a very powerful emotion that can exist between siblings, could be considered a subset of "fear." Jealousy stems from insecurities of not being "good enough," of not being deserving of love, etc. These insecurities are essentially based in fear (i.e. "I'm afraid that I'm not *good enough*").

Now, when we look at these five emotions, fear, anxiety, and anger tend to be the ones that produce the most problematic behaviors. Anxiety can be considered a subset of fear, but anxiety, as its own emotion, will play a bigger role in future chapters, so I want to make sure we have a firm understanding of this emotion on its own. We will be looking at "natural anxiety" in specific and understanding how this ties into the need for structure, discipline, and so on, in the home. So, let's begin and tackle anxiety, along with fear, next.

7.1 Anxiety & Fear

Anxiety is a fairly complex emotion. Some people will use the term "nervous" to reflect this feeling. As mentioned previously, anxiety is actually a type of "fear" response in the body. Think about the last time you felt anxious or nervous about something. Did you feel your stomach tossing and turning? Were you breathing faster or shallower? Did your heart rate increase? Now, think about the last time you felt scared? I guarantee your stomach was turning, your breath quickened, and your heart began to race. You have the same physical response to anxiety as you do with fear. That is because these two emotions release the same stress hormone in your body, thereby producing the same effect, known as your "Fight or Flight" response. So, what separates these two emotions? Other than the difference in the type of thought that triggers the feeling, they are the same. We may say we are "scared" about an upcoming exam, or we might say we are "nervous" or "anxious" about it. In the end, these emotions are really identical twins; same DNA, different names and personalities.

So, what kind of behaviors are produced in children by fear and anxiety? All sorts of behaviors come to play, depending on the thought that triggered the emotion. You might have *secretive* behaviors, such as hiding objects, isolative behaviors, or even lying. You could see your child running away from situations (figuratively and literally) or crying. You might also get an anger response, such as tantruming (we'll talk more about this later in this chapter). These behavioral responses often result from **natural anxiety**.

Natural Anxiety in Children

I think we can all agree that children do not hold a place of power in any known society. Adults have that place, not children. Infants are at the mercy of their parents or caregivers, and are helpless for quite some time. In fact, most kids need adults to assist them in most things until the age of five or six, when they finally begin functioning more independently. That doesn't mean, however, that our children don't need our help past the age of six. I guarantee we all know at least one teenager who needs help every day with something! (*"Mom! I can't find my shoes!"* Sound familiar at all???) For all children, and especially young children, *natural anxiety* is what helps to keep them safe. It is the emotion that triggers them to be fearful of strangers, to stay close to mommy or daddy, and to be suspicious of possible poisons. (*"Ewww! Is that a vegetable?!?"*) But how did this natural anxiety develop and why?

These questions are best answered when we consider an evolutionary perspective. All human beings are animals and mammals. Instead of talking about humans, let's talk about other mammals, such as zebras or lions. Most mammals are pack animals or travel in herds. There is typically a leader (usually male) and several females with their young. Young zebras typically stay very close to their mothers. They may play with others, but never far from their mothers. Why? They are prey animals, and have a normal, instinctual anxiety about predators. Wandering too far from the herd leaves them vulnerable to predators, such as lions. The same is true for lion cubs. Although they are predatory animals, they are still vulnerable to other predators, such as hyenas, and need their mother for protection. For both of these animals, the mother is also the source of food. To lose her means to lose their source of nutrition, and thus, guarantees their starvation and eventual death.

Finally, what about strangers? Both of these animals are led by male leaders. When a new male arrives, he must challenge the current leader, and the two must battle. If the newcomer wins, he takes over and will kill all the young. Mothers will do their best to protect their young, but often aren't able to. As such, "the stranger" signals impending doom for the babies. This is true for lions, zebras, and most mammals.

So, now that we've had a zoology lesson, what does this have to do with human beings? Well, human beings are considered mammals and, as such, it would make sense that our own young would still have very primitive emotional responses. As infants, we rely on instinct and instinct tells us to stay close to our caregivers. Just like in the animal world, our parents are our source of food, warmth, protection, and comfort. To be abandoned by them would ensure death. So, it is only natural that infants will develop anxiety surrounding the separation of their caregivers. As the child grows, the anxiety will change to match the new circumstances, such as anxiety about getting in trouble or fear of rejection. Just like we have evolved into more sophisticated creatures, so have our anxieties.

7.2 Sadness

No one wants to see their child in a sad mental state. As parents, we always want to see our children happy and healthy, but that isn't always the case. Sadness is a normal emotion that all human beings feel, and our children must learn to *feel* it and effectively cope with it too. Typically, it is a very uncomfortable feeling for people to encounter and, unfortunately, in an effort to comfort others, many of us make matters worse by saying and/or doing the wrong thing. With children, it is no different. I have encountered many parents who shut down their children's emotions without realizing it. This is a topic all on its own, and we will cover this a little later in much more depth. For the purposes of this chapter, we want to look at how sadness affects behavior.

Sadness can develop into chronic conditions such as Persistent Depressive Disorder or Major Depression. In all cases, common behavior in sad or depressed children might be: crying, isolating, poor sleep, low self-esteem, acting "needy," irritability/anger, and tantrums. Most people are surprised when they learn that sadness in children can be expressed as irritability and anger, and they are curious why this is. The reasoning goes back to the point made previously in this chapter, that children are not in a place of power. I think we can all agree that feeling "sad" leaves one feeling vulnerable. If you're a child, you are *already* vulnerable! To feel sad only deepens that sense of vulnerability, making you feel even more powerless in your life. As such, children would rather shift into a "stronger" emotion (typically anger), which feels less vulnerable and more powerful. It is important to note that this shift in emotion is a subconscious one and that it occurs so easily in children (and adults!) because anger is a "secondary" emotion.

7.3 Anger

Anger is a special emotion, and a complex one too. Something that I frequently teach my clients in therapy is that anger is a secondary emotion, typically caused by fear, hurt, or frustration, or some combination thereof. Think of it this way, anger is like a pot of water. The water cannot boil on its own; it needs a heating element. Imagine then, this pot of water on the stove with flames warming the water, slowly bringing it to a boil. In this analogy, you are the pot, the water is your level of anger, and the flames are the emotions: Fear, Frustration, and Hurt (i.e. Primary Emotions).

Anger as a Secondary Emotion

As you experience a primary emotion, such as frustration, you begin "heating" the anger inside you (i.e. the water). Eventually, these emotions can become too great, causing you to become overwhelmed, and thus, boil over (or having an anger outburst). This concept of "anger as a secondary emotion" can be hard to grasp, and I am often challenged by my clients in therapy on this one. In therapy, I usually give them examples of how each one of these emotions turn into anger. Let's look at an example:

Jim and his 5-year-old, Lilly, are at the park. Jim instructs Lilly to "stay where I can see you," and then goes to sit on a bench and check-out social media on his phone while Lilly plays. He continuously looks up to check on her, smiles and waves, and then goes back to his phone. After a few moments, he looks up and realizes that Lilly is no longer on the playground. Jim looks around, and when he realizes that she is nowhere to be seen, he gets up and begins searching the park. After several minutes, Jim's heart begins to race as he realizes he can't find Lilly. Suddenly, he is tapped on the shoulder behind him.

"Excuse me, is this your daughter?"

Jim turns to find Lilly, safe and sound. "Yes, thank you." As the stranger leaves, Jim raises his voice, firmly stating, "Lilly! Where were you! I told you to stay where I could see you! I thought something happened to you!"

"I'm sorry Daddy. Don't be mad, please! I was chasing a butterfly...."

Looking at this example, I think it is easy to see that Jim is angry with Lilly for not following directions. If we look deeper, however, we can see that Jim is not simply angry, he was scarred. When he realized he could not find his daughter, he feared the worst. We might also say that Jim felt frustrated with Lilly because she did not stay within his view. Hopefully, with this example, you can see how anger is really triggered by primary emotions.

Now that we've come to understand the basic emotions of children and have connected some of the typical behaviors you will see, it's time to move forward. In the next chapter, we are going to continue our conversation about emotions. We'll take a look at emotion regulation, distress/frustration tolerance, and review ways you can help your child build these vital skills.

8

Emotion Regulation

Most individuals don't know what "emotion regulation" means, but it's a really important concept to understand, especially when we're speaking about children. Essentially, **emotion regulation** is the way a person controls and/or regulates the emotion they are experiencing at any given time. In order to help us better understand this concept, I want you to think of a stove. On a stove you have a knob that typically has the words "low," "medium," and "high" written on it. This knob is your gas regulator which controls the heat setting on your appliance. If you own a really expensive stove, the gas regulator on it is a very precise mechanism giving you a good range in heat. As such, turning the knob slowly will either decrease or increase the heat of your stove at a very precise rate. On the other hand, if you have a cheaper appliance, your regulator is not as precise and sensitive to the turn of the knob. As such, when you turn that knob, even slightly, you might get a giant flame that seems to burst out of nowhere, or you might get no flame at all. On this stove, it is hard to find those medium-high or medium-low temperatures. Human beings are similar to stoves and these regulators when it comes to emotion.

Folks who have great emotion regulation are similar to the "expensive" stove. Their ability to regulate their emotions (or "temperature") is well developed and, as such, they have better control over intense emotions, such as anger. Folks who tend to blow up very easily, are easily offended, or cry often, are similar to the cheaper stove, where they struggle to control the temperature of their appliance. These folks struggle more with emotion regulation. Young children (such as toddlers) and older children (such as those in puberty) tend to have poor emotion regulation. In many ways, emotion regulation is attached to emotional maturity, but other factors, such as personality and temperament, also play a role.

When I work with children who have poor emotion regulation, the two key components to helping them are:

1. Assisting the child in understanding the emotion they are experiencing at any given time
2. Helping them develop ways to cope and calm themselves down when upset

The first part is important because, in order to help prevent anger outbursts or temper tantrums, a child must first be able to tell that they are reaching their point where their pot will boil over. Understanding their emotions, how their emotions play out in their body, as well as being able to label and identify their emotions, goes a great distance in helping children learn how to calm themselves down when upset. The second component, which is the actual act of helping them calm down, is related to teaching them coping skills, or behaviors that they can engage in that help them to de-escalate their own emotional response. Later in this chapter, we will go into more detail on how to teach children the ability to regulate, but first, it is important for parents to understand where a child's emotion regulation comes from.

8.1 The Roots of Emotion Regulation

Essentially, we can break down emotion regulation into two parts: biology and learned behavior (i.e. nature and nurture). Biology consists of the child's natural temperament and personality. Learned behavior consists of what the child has witnessed in the home as appropriate ways to manage different emotions. Both of these concepts are not new at this point to you since we have discussed them in depth in previous chapters. As a reminder, however, remember that temperament and personality are essentially the material that you as a parent have been given to work with when it comes to raising and molding that human being. **Modeling**, which relates to the second point mentioned here, is the tool that you have at your disposal to shape and mold those materials that you have in front of you. It is important to understand that you can have a child who naturally has an explosive disposition and still be able to mold that child, via modeling and parental intervention, into a child who is better able to manage his or her emotions on a day-to-day basis.

As parents we should never use our child's temperament or their personality as an excuse for the poor behavior they display or for their inability to regulate emotions. This point goes back to our parenting philosophies we discussed in the first chapter, where I mentioned that you must believe that your child is inherently good or at the very least neutral. If you believe that your child is just "bad," then you must also believe that there is nothing that you can do to help your child, and this is simply not true. It may not be easy, but in my work with disturbed and destructive children, I have come to see and believe that any child can be taught how to better manage their emotions and display them appropriately.

Through this chapter, I will be teaching you more about what emotion regulation looks like and then how you can help your child learn appropriate ways to display difficult emotions, such as anger.

8.2 Poor Emotion Regulation

In order to better understand where you want to go with a child's emotion regulation, you must first understand where your child is at. I'm a big believer in this and believe that all human growth starts with understanding where you currently are in your parenting journey. As such, I'm going to help you better understand what would be considered poor emotion regulation in children.

With young children, temper tantrums are commonly witnessed as poor emotion regulation. Temper tantrums can also be considered normal human development for young children between the ages of 18 months and approximately 3 ½ years old. This time is frequently known as the "Terrible Two's," but can often persist a little after the age of 2. But what is considered a temper tantrum? In my experience, the definition of a "temper tantrum" changes from family to family. I have seen parents label a child crying because they are upset a "temper tantrum," and I have seen parents label a child who has thrown himself on the ground as having a "temper tantrum."

Alicia Lieberman describes a temper tantrum as a child throwing themselves on the ground while crying and screaming uncontrollably (61). For myself, I like to define a **temper tantrum** as an emotional reaction that is beyond what would be considered "normal" for that particular event. For example, a 10-year-old child who is told they need to wait one minute while a parent finishes a task before they can start a new activity may very well become upset, frown, and talk back. This, although annoying, is not necessarily a temper tantrum because it is not a reaction that is "beyond" what would be considered "normal" given the child's age and developmental level. Now, if in this same scenario the child were to throw themselves on the ground and begin screaming and kicking, that would be considered a temper tantrum because the reaction is beyond what would be considered "normal." The reason why the second is considered a temper tantrum as opposed to the first is because, in the first, the child is merely displaying displeasure with the response received from their parent. It is important to remember that our children are allowed to feel anger and to be upset when they are not getting what they want. In the second scenario, the reaction seems a bit much for a child who was told to just wait a minute. Typically, most mental health professionals will consider a tantrum to consist of a child who throws himself on the floor, kicks, screams, hits, and cries uncontrollably for a period of time that seems out of the ordinary.

Now, many parents want to know where temper tantrums come from, why do they happen, and how can they prevent them. As I have stated previously, I truly believe that you must know where you are coming from in order to know where you have to go. In my experience working with child behavior, this notion is absolutely true. A huge component of changing behavior comes from understanding why your child is engaging in that behavior to begin with. What purpose does the behavior serve for your child?

There are three primary reasons why a child will engage in tantrum-like behavior. For your child, the reason may be one or any combination of these. We will discuss each one individually in order to gain a deeper understanding of the problem at hand. It is also important to note that, although I am talking about temper tantrums, which can be considered typical behavior for young children, these reasons that we are about to discuss can be just as true for teens or older children who engage in anger outbursts.

Lack of Ability to Communicate

I think we can all agree that young children typically lack a full and varying vocabulary. Although they may be able to get general points across to people, they still lack enough sophistication and a broad enough vocabulary to really express themselves. Because the child can't effectively communicate their inner experience, they become frustrated. If we remember back in our previous chapters on anger and emotions, I mentioned that anger is a secondary emotion fueled by frustration, hurt, fear, or some combination of these. In this situation, when a child has difficulty expressing him or herself, they become frustrated because they cannot vocalize and express their frustration in a way that caregivers are able to adequately understand and address. This then results in tantruming behavior. Furthermore, this frustration also comes with feelings of being misunderstood. It's easy to see that, if a child can't explain exactly what it is that they need or want from a caregiver, and a caregiver is left to guessing and trying to decipher what it is that the child is trying to say, the child will feel misunderstood by the caregiver and, thus, lead to increased frustration and eventually some sort of anger outburst.

Teens frequently feel misunderstood and, as a result, will oftentimes shut their emotions in (i.e. internalize emotion), and will not speak to their parents about what it is they are internally experiencing. Instead, they tend to speak more to friends, feeling that their friends have a better ability to understand them and their internal emotional experience. This buildup of internal emotion, however, can create a volcanic effect where too much pressure builds within the teen, and they explode in an outburst of emotion. At times, this explosion of emotion may be witnessed as crying spells but is more frequently witnessed as an anger outburst.

Poor Modeling

One of the more consistent themes of this book is the importance of good modeling coming from parents to their children. When it comes to emotion regulation, this is no different. Frequently in therapy, I have treated children who engage in temper tantrums or anger outbursts, but the child isn't the only one in the family doing these things. The parent is also guilty of these behaviors. Take a second to reflect on yourself.

Do you ever storm out of a room when upset? Have you ever run out of the house to take a walk when angry? Do you ever yell at your partner in heated arguments? Have you ever caught yourself making statements such as, "He's such an idiot," "I don't know why I'm with him," or "I should leave… these people are useless"? Have you ever engaged in name-calling towards your partner, or perhaps the co-worker who has upset you?

The reality is, most parents are guilty of these behaviors during periods of high stress, which would include anger. If you truly believe that you have never behaved in this way, consider asking a family member or a friend whom you trust. Let that person give you an objective opinion on how you act during times of high stress. You may be surprised to find that you are also guilty of tantrum-like behavior.

It is really important to be able to identify what behaviors we, as parents, are also engaging in that might be influencing our children and showing them that such behaviors are appropriate during periods of high stress. No one is perfect, but identifying these common mistakes allows you to become more aware of yourself. This helps you to develop a game plan on what you need to do in order to be a better example for your children.

Parents are not always to blame for poor modeling. Older siblings and family friends with whom children spend a large amount of time with, grandparents who watch your children after school, or peers can be a poor influence on your children and their behavior. If you know that you are not guilty of engaging in tantrum-like behavior, then you may want to take a second to evaluate who are the significant people in your child's life whom they spend a lot of time with. How do those people respond during fits of anger or high stress? If these individuals do not seem to be the problem, it might be time to start looking at your child's friends and determining if these peers are appropriate social companions for them.

Temperament

Temperament can be defined as an individual's natural way of responding to events and their behavioral style (Santrock 136). It is your base from which you act and react. Some folks have a very mild, easy going personality and/or temperament, whereas other people may be a bit more spirited and intense in the way they act and react to situations. Temperament is going to play a big role in how you act under times of stress, and it is no different for your child. Researchers have worked hard to define and classify temperament. Although there are a few different classifications for temperament, the most well-known are the ones suggested by Alexander Chess and Stella Thomas (218 - 226). They identified 3 basic temperament styles:

1. **Easy Child**- Children with this temperament are generally happy and positive children. They adapt to changes in their lives without too much trouble, adopt new experiences with ease, and quickly settle into new routines as infants.
2. **Difficult Child**- A child that would fall into this category is a little more difficult (as the name implies). Children in this category cry frequently, struggle with changes in their lives, and tend to react negatively. Their moods can be intense. Children who fall into this category are more prone to temper tantrums and/or anger outbursts.
3. **Slow-to-Warm-Up Child**- Children with this temperament are typically seen as "low energy." They can be somewhat negative, struggle to adopt changes to their lives or daily routine and have mild moods.

There is little you can do to change a child's temperament, but you can help teach your child ways to manage their temperament during times of anger and stress. This goes along with teaching your child how to regulate themselves during these situations. This is going to be a big focus of this chapter later on.

8.3 Older Children and Teens

We've discussed young children and those pesky temper tantrums that have most parents feeling overwhelmed when it comes to raising toddlers. Now the time has come to discuss older kids and their infamous anger outbursts. My guess is, you won't be surprised to hear that anger outbursts are nothing other than "big kid" temper tantrums. They can feel more intense, but that is only because they are coming from older children. Since older children have better vocabulary, anger outbursts may consist of more verbal threats, hateful language, or making statements that are intended to hurt your feelings. In the end, however, this is no different than your toddler screaming at the top of their lungs because they couldn't have another cookie.

For older children, anger outbursts are caused for the same reasons as temper tantrums, but there are a few differences. The main difference is that, unlike toddlers, teens have a full range of vocabulary and a deeper understanding of emotions. At this point, your child should have also developed some coping skills that they can use to regulate themselves under times of stress. This doesn't mean that your child is immune to anger outbursts, but there should be fewer anger outbursts in a situation such as this. As a therapist, I've worked with many older children who fail to learn adequate coping skills, or perhaps they were taught that screaming and yelling were an appropriate way to manage anger via modeling from the important caregivers in their lives. In these situations, you may find your older child engaging in anger outbursts. Similar to young children, teens often feel misunderstood, which then produces frustration that causes anger. Teens frequently feel as though no one is listening to them, or that their opinion, thoughts, and feelings are not important. This leads to hurt, frustration, and fear, which causes that pot of anger to over boil.

In my extensive work with young men in residential treatment facilities, I quickly came to see that fear of being unlovable, being unworthy of care, or a fear of never finding a stable living environment frequently caused these boys to lash out in extremely aggressive physical and verbal behaviors. Residential treatment facilities are a prime example of how young individuals who feel misunderstood and unwanted will channel those emotions into more powerful ones, such as anger. In many ways, anxiety, which is just a form of fear, is a root cause of anger outbursts.

Some teens don't engage in anger outbursts but, rather, engage in other risky behaviors to help regulate their emotions. Some of these behaviors might be running away from home, engaging in non-suicidal self-harm (such as cutting behaviors or picking at the skin), or they may have suicidal thoughts. All of these are a prime example of a child who is struggling to regulate their emotions, and is seeking a way to discharge all of that pent-up energy, such as fear and hurt. This, in turn, helps them to feel more emotionally balanced.

In the sections to follow in this chapter, we will be discussing the nervous system and how some emotions, such as anxiety, can cause a fight or flight response in the body, which then gets stuck and needs to be discharged via a healthy coping mechanism. Towards the end of the chapter, we will discuss ways to teach your child developmentally appropriate coping skills that they can use to help regulate their emotions during times of stress.

8.4 Healthy Emotion Regulation

For the past 2 decades, there have been changes in how mental health professionals view trauma. Without going into the biology of it all, the basics are that the nervous system reacts to external stressors with the **Fight or Flight Response**.

Essentially, whenever you encounter a situation that your brain interprets as potentially threatening, your brain signals the body to engage in a Fight or Flight response. This causes a chain reaction that prepares your body to either fight for your life or run for your life. Now, your brain doesn't always interpret situations accurately. The part of your brain that is assessing potential life or death situations is a fairly primitive part and it doesn't interpret "gray areas" very well. It is very black and white. An example might be a fight with a spouse.

During a fight with your spouse, your brain is going to interpret the situation as a "dangerous" one. This, in turn, is going to trigger that Fight or Flight response. This is why you'll feel that surge of energy (i.e. adrenaline) or you might feel your heart pounding or stomach churning. These are all normal, bodily reactions caused by the Fight or Flight response. I think we can all agree that a fight with your spouse isn't a life or death situation (unless you are in a Domestic Violence relationship), but your brain doesn't see that this situation is a "gray area." Your brain just recognizes that this situation is a high intensity situation and that you are at a potential risk. In turn, your body kicks in with the Fight or Flight response.

I don't want to go too far into the neuroscience of this process. For more information, you can always check out the *Art of Parenting Workbook*. For now, the important thing for you to understand is that we all have this survival mechanism in our bodies, and we all utilize this system automatically. This is a "survival" reflex and it can't be controlled. BUT... you can recognize it and learn to coach yourself through it.

Now that you know about this Fight or Flight response, what does it have to do with emotion regulation? Well, when we go into a Fight or Flight response, we are functioning from that primitive place in our brain. We are not in great control of ourselves, and this is why we may say things or do things that we end up regretting later. Now that we have this foundational knowledge, let's narrow the view a bit and look at how the Fight or Flight response applies to our children.

I think we can all agree that when our children have temper tantrums or anger outbursts, they aren't regulating their emotions AT ALL! And you are accurate in this thought process. When our children are in that headspace, they are not regulated, they are not thinking clearly, and they are very much in a Fight or Flight response. In fact, they are (what I like to call) *past their point of no return.*

The Point of No Return

Have you ever watched a movie where the main character comes up to a fork in the road? One of the paths leads to this bright and sunny looking trail and the other path leads to this dark and scary forest. And of course, the scary forest usually has some signs out that say *Beware, Turn Back,* or *Enter at Your Own Risk.* Can you picture that scene in your mind's eye? Hold that image for a moment, because we are going to need it.

When we find ourselves in situations where we are becoming emotional and reactive, our body usually gives us little signs that we are getting upset. This might be an increase in heart rate, ringing in your ears, heavy breathing, tingling in the arms or legs, etc. It's a little different for all of us, but we all have some of these bodily signs that we are starting to get angry. This is the fork in the road. When you start sensing all of these bodily signs, these are your *warning* signs. They are the *Beware* and *Turn Back* signs that your body is screaming at you, letting you know that you are starting to go down into the scary forest of emotional meltdown!

If you ignore these warning signs and choose to continue down the same path, you will approach your *Point of No Return*. This is the point in the story where the main character has gone down the path of the scary forest, and he's too deep into the forest to turn around. Perhaps he goes into the forest and then tries to turn back but realizes he's lost. Or maybe he's in the forest and the villain has circled behind him, blocking his path of escape. Whatever the reason, the hero of the story is now stuck in the forest, and the only way out is to continue forward. This is the *Point of No Return*, where there *is* no turning back.

When you ignore your body's warning signs, and you keep going down the scary forest path, you eventually come to a point where there is no turning back. Your emotions have become too great and your primitive brain (sometimes referred to as the Reptilian Brain) has taken over. You are fully engaged in your Fight or Flight response. That's it… game over! You've gone past the *Point of No Return*. For your child, this is their temper tantrum, their anger outburst, etc.

Hopefully that analogy of the scary forest helps you to understand what happens to you when you lose your "cool" as a parent, but also what happens to your child when they have a meltdown. Essentially, this lack of emotional control is the result of a Fight or Flight response. For some individuals, their Fight or Flight response is triggered very easily and quickly. This is usually an individual who has a low **frustration tolerance** (also known as *distress tolerance*). For individuals whose Fight or Flight response is *not* easily triggered, they have a high frustration tolerance.

Elaine Miller-Karas is the author of *Building Resilience to Trauma: The Trauma and Community Resiliency Models*, and in her book, she discusses the **Resilient Zone**. She explains that when we are in this zone, we are able to effectively navigate the twists and turns that come up in our daily life. We are flexible and are able to easily adapt to the challenges the might arise (8). In Elaine's model, this emotional meltdown is when a person has been "bumped out" of their Resilient Zone. Now, her book goes on to talk about how being bumped out of the Resilient Zone leads to trauma. We're not going to go down that road of discussing trauma because that's a whole book in itself and it deviates from the purpose of this book, which is to help you understand the basic mechanisms of successful parenting. What's important for you to understand right now is that we all have a Resilient Zone. In order to understand the concept of the Resilient Zone, let's use an analogy which I like to refer to as your *Emotional Cup*.

Your Emotional Cup

Imagine that you have a cup, and this cup is your capacity to tolerate stress. Whenever you encounter a stressful event, water is poured into this cup. The more stressful the event, the more water is poured in. The longer the stressful event lasts, the more water is poured in. As such, we can see that the magnitude of a stressful event, as well as its chronicity (meaning how long the stressor is happening for), the more water is placed into your cup. The problem with this is that we all have a limit. Our cup can only take so much fluid before the water overflows and spills out everywhere. This is equivalent to being bumped out of our Resilient Zone or going past our point of no return.

In order to avoid this scenario, logic would tell us that we need to empty out that cup before we reach this point. The question then is, how do we empty our emotional cup before it overflows?

Whenever you engage in self-care or utilize healthy coping skills, you pour out some (or all) of the water that has been collected in this cup. You empty this water out in a controlled way which allows you to stay in control of your emotions and actions. When you are in control of your emotions and actions, you are functioning within your Resilient Zone. This means that you have not come to that fork in the road that leads to the scary forest OR you have chosen to take the bright and sunny path, effectively avoiding the scary forest.

I had a client once who asked me, "What happens if my cup isn't an 8oz glass but a little Dixie cup?" I have to admit, I laughed and we both enjoyed the humor of this question together. But it was an excellent question! The reality is, the "size" of our Emotional Cups are all different. Some of us have a big 32oz cup and some of us have a tiny Dixie cup. This is our "nature," our biology.

Some of us are born with a better capacity to handle stress, and some of us are born with a much smaller capacity, but this doesn't mean we are doomed to constantly being overwhelmed by life and always overflowing! You have the ability to empty your cup out regularly in a controlled manner with good self-care. BUT... you also have the ability to grow the size of your cup over time. You can trade your Dixie cup out for a BIG 32oz one, but it takes A LOT of personal development and time to accomplish this. It means taking a good look at your own emotional baggage, unpacking some of those hurts, fears, traumas, and whatever other skeletons in your closet to successfully grow your cup.

Now, just like you have an Emotional Cup, so does your child, and children (by their very nature) are more likely to have their cup overflow much more easily than adults. This is because children have low frustration tolerance and lack the skills needed to empty out their cup in a controlled way. This is where the parenting part comes in. As the parent, part of your job is to help your child learn ways to empty their cup in a controlled way. You may do this through modeling healthy coping skills, teaching your child coping skills, and/or helping them engage in regular self-care activities. With that said, let's look further into what healthy coping skills are and how to do them so that you can begin emptying your own cup AND help your child empty their cup too!

8.5 Healthy Coping Skills

Let's shift gears and begin looking at what coping skills are. I think this term sounds elusive. It leaves people wondering how you gain coping skills and utilize them effectively. We're going to break this whole thing down into 2 parts:

1. Defining coping skills and explaining how you use them
2. Provide a list of potential coping skills with directions for their use

By the end of this chapter, you'll gain some new skills for yourself and your child!

What are Coping Skills & How Do You Use Them?

Coping skills are different actions an individual can take in order to help them manage difficult emotions such as anger, anxiety, or sadness. Coping skills can help a person weather stressful life events to help minimize the psychological negative impact that the stressor may have on the individual. Using coping skills on a regular basis will help you empty your cup in a controlled manner when used frequently throughout the day or week. Using coping skills will also help to keep you from getting to your *Point of No Return* when you use them during a high stress situation. This brings us to the topic of how do you best use coping skills to make them most effective?

Use Them Regularly

The biggest mistake I see clients make when trying to use coping skills is that they only use them when they are already upset. Doing this is setting you up for failure. Here's the secret to using coping skills *effectively*: You have to use them regularly when you are *not* upset! This may seem counter-intuitive, but it's the truth nonetheless.

Without going too far into the weeds with this topic, let me explain why using a coping skill regularly makes it more effective. Some coping skills, such as deep breathing, will force your body to slow down when used correctly. This helps to combat the Fight or Flight response. By practicing regularly, your brain forms an association with the skill as being soothing. It's the same concept behind bedtime routines.

When your child was a baby, you probably had a bedtime routine. Some routines are elaborate with lullabies, stories, and snuggles before bed. Others are simpler with just a bath, a kiss, and then lights out. Whatever your routine was, it helped to put your baby to sleep at night. Did you ever wonder why? It's because your child's brain formed an association between that routine and sleep. After you repeated this routine for several nights on a regular basis, your child's brain began to realize that the routine meant it was time to go to bed. As such, the brain began the process of making your child sleepy.

There's a lot that happens when your brain winds down for the night (a lot of biology with different chemicals increasing and decreasing in the brain). That bedtime routine helped to signal to the brain that the time had come for that process to start. But it takes several nights of doing the same thing every single night in order for the brain to make that connection. Once it does, however, your bedtime routine becomes a powerful ally against bedtime battles.

Brain associations are common with many things we do. Our brain is biologically wired to form all of these connections in order to make life easier for us. In short, our brain LOVES routine and structure. The more structure and routine we have in our lives, the safer and more in control we feel in our life, producing a deep sense of security. That's what our kids love too!

When you begin practicing your coping skills on a regular basis during a calm and relaxed state, you help your brain to form an association between that skill and feeling relaxed. That association gets stronger and more powerful every time you do it because it strengthens those neural pathways in the brain. This means that when things get really tough suddenly, and you need your coping skills to help you calm down, it's going to be much more effective! Why? Because, not only are you engaging in a technique that is forcibly helping your body to slow down, but you've harnessed the power of brain associations to boost the calming effect that skill has on your emotions!

Practicing your coping skill regularly is going to have a dual effect in that, not only will you be forming that brain association, but you will also be emptying your *Emotional Cup* on a regular basis. Engaging in this practice means that you will feel overwhelmed less often and have a higher tolerance for stress and frustration. Don't be shocked if you encounter other beneficial effects too, such as lowered blood pressure!

Apply Your Skills Before Your Cup is Too Full

Sometimes, even though you've been practicing your coping skills every day, you still might find yourself overwhelmed. This is because the stressors you are encountering in your life are filling your cup faster than your daily routine is helping to empty it. It might also be because the stressor is a HUGE one, like a sudden death or traumatic event. In these situations, you need to begin applying your coping skills immediately.

I mentioned earlier in this chapter that your body gives off little warning signs to let you know that you are approaching your *Point of No Return*. This is the point where your cup is almost filled to the brim but isn't overflowing yet. Learning to recognize what those signs are is a key step in mastering stressful emotions. We all have these little warning signs. For me, I usually feel the turning of my stomach, like butterflies swirling around, which is then followed by a shot of adrenaline that I sense in my chest first (like a shot of warmth spreading outward from the center of my chest). When I sense these bodily signals, I know my body is preparing for a Fight or Flight response, which means my cup is filling up and I am approaching my *Point of No Return*. When I feel these sensations, I know it's time to start applying my coping skills. The same goes for you and your child!

Begin taking the time to learn what your warning signs are and help your child to learn their own. Being aware of what your body is doing is a monumental step in helping to master emotional regulation. Once you've learned your body's warning signs, you'll want to begin applying your coping skills right then and there. Whatever skills you've been practicing, start applying those to help you stay in control of yourself. If you notice your child's warning signs, instruct them to use their skills too! Do it with them and model to them how to use these skills during troubling times. This will help keep your child from boiling over into a rage or deep depression and is key to building a resilient child.

Layer Coping Skills during High-Stress Events

Sometimes, the stressor we are encountering is just too great. You might be engaging in your technique, but it doesn't seem to be calming you down enough. When this happens, individuals will give up. No single coping skill is so powerful that it can bring instant, lasting emotional relief during a high stress event. In situations like these, the secret is to layer different coping skills until you have regained control of yourself.

Let's look at this a little differently and consider a stressful emotion, such as anger, on a scale from 1 to 10. Ten is when the Emotional Cup has overflowed and you are past your *point of no return*. A 7 or 8 on this scale might be when you begin to see your warning signs. A 5 or 6 is where you might feel emotional distress and you know you are getting angry, but your body isn't starting to kick in that Fight or Flight response yet. You are still level-headed enough to make good decisions and assess the consequences of your behavior. The numbers 1 through 4 on this scale represent differing levels of stress, but all minor enough that they are easily controlled. The situation might be considered nothing more than an annoyance or frustrating barrier.

If you are expressing stress on that 1-4 scale, a coping skill might not even be necessary to use, but can be effective in reducing the stress. Once you reach 5-7, you should begin applying your coping skills, and you should find that they are helping you in reducing your rating or at least maintaining it so that your cup doesn't overflow. As you approach 7 - 9, you'll find that one coping skill will rarely do the trick. It's fairly ineffective, and this, in turn, will leave you discouraged. In this situation, you should begin using multiple skills to help maintain and reduce your stress.

For example, say you are at a 9, so you begin with a Deep Breathing technique. This brings you down to an 8, which isn't a huge improvement. So, you switch to Visualization which maintains you at an 8. Then you apply Grounding which brings you to a 7, and then you try Deep Breathing again which calms you further to a 6. This is called **Layering Coping Skills**, and it is very effective. It's not fast by any means, but it *does* work. The key is having a variety of coping skills that you have practiced over time to make them effective for you. Then, you must have enough discipline to apply those skills over and over again until you are back in control (around 4 or 5). Layering coping skills is effective for multiple reasons:

- You are continuously forcing your body to calm down through relaxation techniques, which helps to stall out the Fight or Flight response
- You are forcing your mind to shift its focus from the problem/stressor to the coping skill, which helps to keep you from reigniting your Fight or Flight response

- In general, the Fight or Flight response is a temporary, short-lived effect on the body, so layering coping skills helps you to regulate your emotions while riding out that response.

These 3 points are the *how* of coping skills. Many individuals have coping skills, but few use them correctly or appropriately. If you can begin mastering these 3 steps, you'll be more efficient at emptying your cup regularly. This will help you be a better parent because you'll be in more control of your emotions, less stressed, less burned out, and a lot less likely to yell all the time. Even more inspiring is that you'll be modeling these same skills to your kids! That means they'll start following your lead and using coping skills effectively to help themselves when they begin to feel overwhelmed by emotion. Furthermore, because you'll be such an expert at it, you'll be able to coach them through it, which will benefit your Parent-Child Relationship. It's a total win-win for everyone!

Your Family's Coping Skills Toolkit

At this point, we've dived into a lot of different topics surrounding emotion regulation, but now we're going to learn some skills. I've already named a few in the section above, so you should have an idea of what coping skills look like. In this section, we are going to break down coping skills into 2 categories: Internal versus External coping skills.

1. **External Coping Skills** - Skills that fall in this category exist outside of you or require a physical object to work. For example, a stress ball is a well-known and classic stress relief tool. It's an external coping skill because it requires a physical object in order to work.
2. **Internal Coping Skills** - These are skills that don't require anything but you! Nothing else is required. Examples include Progressive Muscle Relaxation, Deep Breathing, Meditation, Visualization, Mindfulness, etc. Unlike external skills, internal ones utilize only your mind.

When I work with clients, I require that my clients master at least 1 external and 2 internal coping skills throughout treatment. There are good reasons why I require this. To begin, in order to layer coping skills in a high stress situation, you need multiple skills. In my work with intensely complex cases, 3 coping skills seems to be the minimum for effective emotion regulation. Mastery of more skills is even better, but 3 will get you by.

You'll notice that I recommend 1 external and 2 internal skills for the initial toolkit. When I worked with troubled teens, they would always question why they needed to have coping skills from both categories, which is a great question! Internal coping skills are the most effective at slowing down your heart rate and helping to stall the Fight or Flight response, but it's really hard to get your mind to focus on something like breathing during a high stress situation. Kids oftentimes lack the discipline over the mind to do this. As such, most kids fail to use their coping skills when they are upset. This is when I came up with the requirement that my teens should master an external coping skill.

External coping skills are not as effective at stalling the Fight or Flight response, but they are much easier to use during high stress events. Since they don't require mastery of the mind, children find external coping skills to be much easier to implement when they are angry or stressed. As such, I coach my clients to use their external coping skill first. As they begin to feel a tiny bit more in control, I coach them to switch to an internal skill, and then to begin layering their skills. In this way, my clients have been able to develop their ability to regulate their emotions effectively. Over time, they can learn new skills, but these 3 coping skills become the foundation to their Coping Skills Toolkit.

Remember, as a parent, we need to be modeling all of these things in order to really help our children learn effective emotion regulation. Do you have healthy coping skills? If you don't, now's the time to start building your own Coping Skills Toolkit. There are so many coping skills out there! In order to help you out, you can check out *The Art of Parenting Workbook* for specific exercises to try, or visit *The Wholistic Family Blog* on my website (kcdreisbach.com) for more articles on coping and wellness.

9

A Wholistic Approach to Discipline

It has been quite the journey, and we are nowhere near being done yet! The time has come to tackle one of the most difficult topics, and that's discipline. Many parents aren't comfortable with discipline because it may bring up painful memories, they may not know how to do it, have limited knowledge of different disciplinary techniques (i.e. timeouts, spankings, removing privileges, etc.), or simply don't like doing it because it makes them feel badly. All of these things tend to give discipline a bad reputation.

By the end of this chapter, you will have a richer and fuller understanding of discipline. You'll be taking a much more wholistic approach that will empower you and give you fresh, invigorating ideas on how to manage your children. To begin, let's start with a new definition and understanding of discipline.

The word discipline comes from the root word *disciple*, which means "to teach." Therefore, **discipline** is the art of teaching our children. That's it! Pretty simple, right? Most people only see discipline as a punishment, but I am going to expand your way of thinking about discipline.

Wholistic Discipline (a component to my Wholistic Parenting approach) consists of love and affection, healthy boundaries, rules and limits, structure, praise, rewards, and consequences. A good disciplinarian has successfully mastered a balance between rewards and consequences, rigidity and flexibility. This is a wholistic approach to discipline. To understand this concept better, we will break it down further into its multiple parts. We will begin with the broader concept of the home environment and then hone it down to the parent-child relationship, which is your interaction with your child every day.

9.1 Home Environment

The home environment consists of three major components:

1. Structure & Routine
2. Rules & Limits
3. Rewards & Consequences

We are going to break down each one and take a closer look at how you can master these parts in your own household.

Structure & Routine

Most parents know that young children thrive on structure and routine. Alicia Lieberman states that routine acts as a container that holds anxiety and uncertainty for kids, and provides them with reassurance and connection with the caregivers that provide this structure for them (220). This, however, isn't just true for young children, it is also true for teens and adults. Human beings do best when they have knowledge about what to expect during different parts of the day. As adults, we feel more in control of our lives when we have some semblance of structure and routine. For children, a lack of structure and routine leads to feelings of insecurity and anxiety, which can produce defiant behaviors, emotional instability (i.e. mood swings), and difficulty transitioning from one event to the next, among other struggles.

A well-balanced, structured home includes set times for work, play, sleep, and family time. Some parents have shared with me in the past that they dislike structured routines for their whole family and life. The main reason being that they want more flexibility in their daily life, and so they prefer not to have structure at all. This, however, is a misconception about what structure is all about.

Having a structured routine for your family does not mean you must be rigid in maintaining this routine. Flexibility is just as important as structure. It is okay to have flexibility in your daily schedule. The point of a structured home is to provide your child with some knowledge of what comes first, next, then after that. Let's look at an example....

Let's say the structure of dinnertime in your family is as follows:

- Saying grace
- Eating the main meal
- Eating dessert
- Cleaning the dinner table

On one day, you may follow this structure, and then the next day, you may need to clean the table first and have dessert afterwards. This is an example of a flexible routine where the family follows a general order of events, but the order is not set in stone. Another example may be one day you serve your child's lunch and then put him down for a nap. On the next day, you put him down for a nap first and *then* feed him lunch. The general routine is still in place where the child is having a nap around lunch time.

Having a routine doesn't mean that you must have a set schedule. You're just looking for a rough sketch of what your daily life looks like for you and your family. Some semblance of structure and routine throughout your day will greatly reduce the frequency and severity of temper tantrums, anger outbursts, and arguing about daily events in your household. Structure and routine help to accomplish this because your child will have less anxiety and feelings of insecurity because he knows what to expect throughout the day.

Rules & Limits

Your home environment should consist of appropriate rules and limits for your children. This includes developmentally appropriate consequences and rewards for different behaviors. The home environment should also consist of healthy boundaries and respect for all individuals in the home. This means that, not only should both parents show respect *towards* one another, but respect should also be demonstrated *towards* each child and *between* each child. Respect and healthy boundaries should be one of the cornerstone foundations to your home environment.

One of my first interventions with families is for parents to create a list of family rules. Then, I advocate for this list to be on display in the home. If you are like most parents (myself included), you've only thought of and enforced a family rule when the situation arose. For example, until your child told his first lie, you probably didn't even think of that as an established *family rule*. Sure, you knew that lying was going to be a *No-No* in your house, but you never actually thought of it, or considered what the consequences for lying would be, until your child told that first lie.

Imagine if our society was run this way. Imagine driving in your car and suddenly being pulled over by the police. They walk to your window and hand you a ticket. When you ask *why*, the officer replies, *"You can't drive during the day with your headlights on."* When you ask *why* again, he simply states, *"That's the rule."* How upset would you be? Not only do you not understand the rule, but you didn't know this was a rule to begin with!

As parents, we are often flying by the seat of our pants, desperately trying to make it through another day. Parenting this way on a regular basis, however, will make it that much harder for you to be consistent in your parenting (something we will tackle a little later in this chapter). It also creates confusion, insecurity, and anxiety for your child because they don't understand what is being expected of them at any given time.

Having established family rules contributes to the structure of your home, and consequently, helps to teach your child how to function in society. The home environment should be a *microcosm* of the larger, outside world. One of our greatest tasks as parents is to prepare our kids to function in the society we have chosen to raise them in. Part of the reason why our society writes down laws is because it eliminates confusion and doubt. Your child's classroom has, without a doubt, a list of classroom rules and expectations. And these rules are probably on display for children to see every single day they walk into the classroom. There is wisdom in this practice, and your household should be no different.

Once again, your home should be a **microcosm**, a miniature version of the outside world. As such, having your "laws" (i.e. family rules) clearly written down and on display for all to see quickly helps to eliminate arguing, confusion and frustration. If your child knows exactly what is expected of him, then there is a higher likelihood that he will follow through with those expectations. Does it mean that he will never break the rules? Of course not!

Consider your own behavior for a moment: Do you still speed on the highways even though you know it's against the law? Of course you do! Chances are, however, that you do it less often and with more caution. *And* if a police officer pulls you over for speeding, you probably won't argue with him. Why? Because you *knew* you were speeding and you *knew* you were breaking the law. The same goes for your child.

Rewards & Consequences

This is a HUGE part of a Wholistic Discipline approach because Rewards & Consequences are at the heart of how you modify and shape your child's behaviors. Do you use Rewards & Consequences in your home? Most parents would answer *yes* to this question, but I'm going to challenge you and argue that you probably *don't*. I'm willing to bet that you *think* you do, but what you are actually engaging in is Bribery & Punishment.

Many parents come to me and share how they are disciplining their kids, thinking that they are engaging in giving rewards for wanted behavior and giving consequences for unwanted behavior. They soon learn from me, however, that what they've been doing all along is bribing their kids and punishing them. When this happens, the kids are actually the ones in control, not the parents.

As I mentioned previously, Rewards & Consequences play a major role in my Wholistic Parenting system. It is also a critical component to a structured, healthy, and loving home. The trick is all in HOW you administer the reward or consequence. It's a fine line, but the difference is made in the details.

Bribing vs Rewarding

If you were to google *bribe* you would get the following definition: "to persuade (someone) to act in one's favor, typically illegally or dishonestly, by a gift of money or other inducement" ("Bribe," def. 1). In this definition, we understand that we are trying to push, beg, and plead for someone to do something for us. Perhaps it is something that they would never do of their own volition. In this situation, the person receiving the bribe has control of the situation.

Let's compare this definition to that of *reward*. Googling this word would turn up the following: "a thing given in recognition of one's service, effort, or achievement" ("Reward," def. 1). In this definition, there is no begging, no pleading, no pushing for the other person to do what we want. The other person has done the work, and we are offering a prize for a job well done. In this situation, the person offering the reward has the control.

So how does this relate to parenting? I mentioned earlier that the difference lies in the details. To help explore this concept, I'm going to provide 2 examples:

Example 1

Mom: "Molly, please turn off your tablet. We have to get ready for school."

Molly ignores Mom and keeps playing.

Mom: Slightly more irritated, "Molly, turn off the tablet now. We are going to be late!"

Molly: "Ok Mom," she says, but continues to play on her tablet anyways.

Mom: "Molly, if you turn your tablet off right now, then I'll let you stay up 15 minutes later tonight."

Molly then proceeds to turn off her tablet.

Example 2

Mom: "Molly, please turn off your tablet. We have to get ready for school."

Molly ignores Mom and keeps playing.

Mom: Slightly more irritated, "Molly, when you turn off the tablet, then I can reward you for following directions."

Molly then proceeds to turn off her tablet.

Mom: "Thank you for following directions. Since you listened to me, I'll allow you to stay up 15 minutes past your bedtime."

Take a moment to see if you can tell which example is "Bribing" and which example is "Rewarding." If you were able to do that, are you able to understand why? Let's start by identifying which one is the *bribe* and which one is the *reward*. Example 1 is the *bribe*, which means Example 2 is the *reward*. But why? What are the details that make these examples different?

Closer Look at Example 1: The Bribe

Hopefully you can feel that Molly is the one in control of this situation from beginning to end. The primary issue is Mom's word choice. When it comes to *bribing* vs *rewarding*, those fine details have to do with semantics. Words have great power in parenting, and you're going to want to harness the power of words to your advantage!

In Example 1, Mom says:

> *"Molly, if you turn your tablet off right now, then I'll let you stay up 15 minutes later tonight."*

She has engaged in an *If-Then* sentence structure that sets up the bribe. Think of other examples like this:

- "If you stop tantruming right now, then I'll give you a cookie."
- "If you behave for me in the store, then I'll buy you something."
- "If you do your homework, then I'll let you have dessert tonight."

Sometimes, bribes can be more obvious, usually because we are desperate:

- "Please stop screaming!! If you stop screaming, then I'll give you candy?!? What about a toy?!?"

When we bribe, the kid is in complete control of the situation. And, every time you bribe, you shift the power differential in your household. This means that the authority and power shifts from the parent to the child. (This was one of the fundamentals to our Parenting Philosophy in Chapter 1.) The more often you do this, the more often your child has the power. Overtime, if done frequently enough, that power shift becomes permanent, and the child loses respect for the parent.

Closer Look at Example 2: The Reward

At first glance, you might argue that Mom is still engaging in bribery. But I'm going to show you that fine detail that makes Mom retain the control in this situation.

> *"Molly, when you turn off the tablet, then I will reward you for following directions."*

In this example, Mom engages in a *When-Then* dynamic. This is slightly different than *If-Then*. WHEN has an unspoken message of, "you *will* do this," whereas IF has the unspoken message of, "you *might* do this." IF offers room for the child to say *no*, whereas WHEN offers no room for disagreement. WHEN is a command. IF is a plea.

Now, this doesn't mean that you can't successfully use *If-Then* statements with your kids. *If-Then* statements can be useful, but when giving commands, we want to make sure we stay in a place of control. As such, these subtle shifts in our language can make a huge difference.

Another difference in Example 2 is that Mom doesn't prematurely "show her cards" to Molly. The second part of her statement simply offers a "reward," but it doesn't give away what that reward is. Here's why that can be important....

Let's say Molly isn't motivated by staying up late. In Example 1, Mom reveals this potential reward to Molly. If Molly wasn't motivated by this reward, she would continue to play on her tablet. Why would she stop for something that doesn't motivate her?

Consider your own behavior for a moment.... Let's say you were offered an additional, monetary incentive at work for working longer hours, and your company shared that the incentive is $1 for an extra hour of work. Chances are, $1 isn't going to motivate you, so you're not going to bother. You'd rather go home. Same idea applies to Molly.

Keeping the reward a mystery means Mom doesn't place herself at risk of Molly snubbing the incentive. Additionally, by revealing the reward at the onset, this opens the table up for bargaining, which is something you don't want as a parent. We will discuss bargaining further along in this chapter.

Consequences vs Punishment

Now that we've figured out how to give effective rewards, our last step is to understand consequences. Just like most parents are engaging in *bribing* instead of *rewarding*, I find many parents are administering *punishments* instead of *consequences*. Like before, the difference lies in the fine lines. To better understand the difference, we will take a closer look at the definitions of each one. By googling each term, the following definitions came up:

Consequence- "a result or effect of an action or condition" ("Consequence," def. 1)

Punishment- "the infliction or imposition of a penalty as retribution for an offense" ("Punishment," def.1)

Hopefully, you can already see the differences between these terms. When I teach this topic to parents in family therapy, I coach them to think of it as a "state of mind."

When we are *punishing* our kids, we are often trying to exert our power over them. There is typically a punitive quality to the disciplinary session and a subconscious desire for retribution. In most cases, if someone were to ask you why you administered that specific punishment and how that punishment links back to the offense, you probably would come up with a pretty lame answer.

When we are administering *consequences*, on the other hand, you know exactly why you are giving that specific consequence and how that consequence links back to your child's offense. The flavor of your disciplinary session is instructional in nature, and links back to our Parenting Philosophy of being your child's first and most influential teacher. Every time your child makes a mistake, it's a teachable moment. If you just administer a consequence but don't talk to your child about what happened and what you expect to see differently, then you lose the opportunity for them to grow and learn. Consequences should always come with a thoughtful discussion between you and your child (I'll give you some tips for this in the *Efficient Communication* section of this chapter). Finally, *consequences* tend to be a natural result of your child's behavior. It makes sense, is logical, and is fair.

Bargaining and Negotiations

Before we move on to the next section of this chapter, I wanted to briefly touch on the topic of bargaining and negotiating with your kids. Have you ever experienced your child negotiating with you? In our previous example, Molly could have easily stated, "*I want to stay up for 30 minutes.*" This becomes a slippery slope when we start talking about power dynamics and control in the home. Just like *If-Then* statements, allowing your child to negotiate or bargain with you about things is not necessarily bad. In fact, it can be a positive thing in your home. But, once again, there is a time and place for these types of dynamics. If you are running late to work/school, the last thing you want to do is get into a bargaining match with your kid.

Bargaining is also a dynamic better reserved for older kids, and not when you are working with toddlers or very young children. In these early years, you are trying to teach your children how to listen and follow directives while establishing the power dynamics in your home. Young children require structure and very clear directives, which is another reason why posted family rules can be so helpful. Negotiating doesn't provide that. It's a gray area, and most young children aren't cognitively ready to understand or manage this type of dynamic.

If you have a child who has proven to be responsible, mature, and well behaved, you can consider allowing bargaining because your child has EARNED it. Children who struggle with healthy boundaries, don't follow directions easily, are immature, or frequently misbehave are not good candidates for negotiating. These children require cleaner, clear lines that are more "black and white." The grey areas of bargaining will only confuse them and set you both up for frequent frustration and arguing.

9.2 Parents

Now that we've looked at the broader environment of your home, it's time to hone down and look at what you, as a parent, need to do to provide wholistic and effective discipline to your children. In this section, we'll look at the following topics:

- Conscientious Parenting vs Reactive Parenting
- Parental Consistency
- Efficient Communication
- Parental Warmth & Affection
- Structure of Disciplinary Sessions

As a parent, you must be consistent, be a clear communicator, firm, warm, and affectionate. We will look at each of these components in greater detail, and you will see how they come together to form a competent, effective, and loving parent.

Conscientious Parenting vs Reactive Parenting

Let me start off by saying that Conscientious Parenting is what you are aiming for, but it is not easy to master. Parenting from this state of mind is hard, and the reality is, none of us can parent from this place ALL THE TIME. It's impossible! We are all human, and we are going to make some mistakes. As long as you are able to accept them and take steps to improve yourself, it will all be ok. With that said, let's take a deeper dive into the differences between Conscientious and Reactive Parenting.

Reactive Parenting is whenever you are parenting from an emotional state (namely when you are angry). When parenting from this place, you are more likely to yell, discipline harshly, and may find yourself saying things like "You are a bad boy," and so on. These are not our finest moments as parents... and we are all guilty of them. We all do this at some point in our parenting career. Just be honest with yourself, recognize it when it happens, and then correct the mistake. The more you do this, the better you will get at it, and the less you'll be parenting from that state of mind.

In contrast, **Conscientious Parenting** is when you are in control of your emotions. Your words and actions are thought out carefully, and your interactions with your child have purpose and meaning to them. During disciplinary sessions, you know exactly why you are giving a specific consequence, and you know how that consequence links back to your child's offense. This doesn't mean that you don't get angry, hurt, frustrated, and so on. Rather, you are *in control* of these emotions, and they do not govern your actions. Conscientious Parenting is a skill, and it takes consistent effort on our part to master it.

Parental Consistency

Parental Consistency is one of those drums that practically every parenting expert beats. Most parenting books speak endlessly on the need to be consistent as a parent, and with good reason! It plays a huge part in behavior modification and, if you can't learn to be consistent as a parent, you'll find that behavioral problems will plague you for years to come!

After working with thousands of families over the course of my career, I've come to see that many parents *know* that they have to be consistent, but often don't *realize* that they aren't. Do you think you are consistent in your own parenting? Have you ever thought about it before? Take a moment to consider it now. Are you a consistent parent?

Most parents don't realize that Parental Consistency has multiple parts. There are 3 parts, in fact, and we're going to take a look at all 3. As a parent, you (and whoever your co-parent is if you have one), must master these 3 components in order to really check this one off. They are:

1. Consistency from day to day
2. Consistency between co-parents
3. Consistency between children

Consistency is critical. As we go through each one, take the time to be honest with yourself. Ask yourself: Is there any way that I can improve with these items?

Consistency Day by Day

Our first component is about being consistent each day of the week. This means that if you have a specific rule in your home that you would like followed, you must be up to the task of enforcing this rule throughout the day and throughout *each* day of the week. On the surface, this component seems extremely basic and easy to follow, but it is one of the trickiest to manage successfully. To illustrate, let's look at an example:

> It is Saturday morning, and you have a rule of "no jumping on the couch." As your child races to the living room to begin his day, he immediately hops onto the sofa with glee and begins bouncing. As you pour your cup of coffee, you give him a warning to stop bouncing on the couch or he'll have a consequence. He stops jumping, but an hour later, begins jumping on the couch again. You give another warning, but this time, he doesn't comply, and you administer a consequence. Five hours later, after spending time outside, he returns to the living room, hopping around once again on the sofa. You give him another warning and end up having to give him a consequence in the end. This time, however, he has a meltdown about the consequence, and your patience is starting to run thin. Imagine that this same routine keeps going on into the night. Now, you are emotionally and physically exhausted, and once again your child is jumping on the sofa.

Most of you know that, no matter how tired you are, you have to be consistent, you have to give out your warnings, and you have to follow through with the appropriate discipline. The truth is, few of us have the energy to keep fighting this tired battle. Furthermore, imagine that this example took place during the week after a long hard day at work. You are even less likely to be consistent and follow through. Hopefully you can see that this component, though easy to understand, is actually much more challenging to meet.

Consistency Between Co-Parents

As a parent, most of us have someone that we are parenting our children with. Your co-parent may be your spouse, your own parents, an aunt or uncle, caregiver, and so on. **Co-parents** are those individuals who are responsible for watching your children a significant amount of the time. If I were to use myself as an example, my co-parents are my husband and my own parents (who babysit daily while we finish our day at work).

For this item, we are looking at consistency among all of your co-parents, especially if you all live in the same household. This means all co-parents share the same expectations of your children and are enforcing the same rules. It doesn't have to be exactly the same, however, just similar. For children, when co-parents stay consistent between each other, our children feel a greater sense of security and stability, and they are better able to meet our expectations of them. When you are consistent from co-parent to co-parent, the likelihood is that your child will be more compliant and meet your expectations more regularly.

Finally, parents must be consistent between one another. This means they must be on the same page and be supportive of one another throughout the disciplinary process. Failure to do so will create alliances between children and specific co-parents. Think of a time when your child might have said, "Well *Dad* lets me do it," or "Grandma *always* lets me have soda with breakfast." These are examples of situations where co-parents are not parenting similarly, and so it leads to alliances between the child and that co-parent. This is an example of *triangulation*, a concept we will discuss in more detail in chapter 10. On the surface, this can seem harmless, but consider how many arguments stem from these types of scenarios. Furthermore, this leads to disruptions in the power dynamics of the home. In these situations, the child may gain more authority than one parent because the child has formed an alliance with the opposite parent. Tackling co-parenting problems is a big task, and we'll dive a little deeper in chapter 10.

Consistency Between Children

Households with multiple children need to establish consistency from one child to the next. This means that if you're disciplining your oldest child for misbehaving, you need to discipline your youngest child for engaging in that same behavior too. Consequences should be given to both children, but they should be developmentally appropriate for your child's age and maturity level. It is important for your children to see the rules applied equally among all children in the home; this demonstrates that you are remaining consistent from child to child. This will decrease the likelihood that your children will experience sibling rivalries. Many sibling rivalries arise because children feel they are being treated differently from their brother and/or sister. As such, this creates feelings of resentment towards their sibling (and sometimes their parents), which then develops into jealousy.

Efficient Communication

Clear communication is an important social skill, plays a vital role in relationships, and is definitely a foundational building block for effective discipline. You have to become a clear communicator. This means that your child must clearly understand what the expectations are for his behavior. Having your family rules written down and on display is one of the ways that you can improve your communication. Not only does it help you be on the same page with your co-parent, but it reduces the "I didn't know" argument that so many older kids *love* using. It's hard to argue that you were unaware of a rule if it is clearly written down and on display. The act of having your family rules written out clearly also helps to improve consistency between co-parents and between children.

Children should also have a clear understanding of what the rewards and consequences are for their behavior. Remember, consequences and rewards should be developmentally appropriate for your child's age and intellectual abilities. When lecturing or communicating to your children, consider the following 8 tips:

1. Go down to your child's eye level

This means that you should either sit on the floor or kneel in front of your child so that you can look at each other in the eye. Do your best to avoid your child having to look up at you and you down at them.

2. Speak slowly, clearly, and calmly

It's important to explain things slowly while also using a firm tone. Try your best to remain calm and keep the volume of your voice down (or to an appropriate level). If your child is upset, screaming at your child will only increase the chances that they will scream right back at you. Modeling calm communication will help your child to calm down too.

3. Use developmentally appropriate words and concepts

Be sure that you break down larger, more complex concepts (if needed) for younger children. I have found that children work well with metaphors. Using metaphors help to create pictures in your child's mind of the lesson you are trying to teach which helps to retain these lessons. If you use a word that seems large or complex, ask your child if they know what the word means. If they say *yes*, ask them to explain the word to you to make sure their understanding of the word/concept is correct. Don't just assume your child understands. Take the opportunity to teach them and help expand their vocabulary!

4. Avoid sarcasm in your communications

Young children don't understand sarcasm well and will most likely be confused by what you are trying to express. Sarcasm will also model poor behavior for your older children and will increase the likelihood that your teen will respond to you with sarcasm in the future. Would you like it if your teen responded to you with sarcasm? Would you consider it disrespectful? Would a teacher at school consider it disrespectful? It's just best practice to avoid this as best as you can during disciplinary sessions.

5. Be specific

When praising your child, be sure to affirm a specific behavior, be specific with the behavior you want replaced, and be specific with the behavior that you want to see instead. The more specific you are and the more consistent you are in being specific, the higher the likelihood you will see an increase or decrease in the behaviors you want changed. *Specificity* is one of the most important parts of being an efficient communicator. Mastering this alone will do wonders to improve your child's behavior and the efficacy of your disciplinary sessions. To really grasp this tip, let's look at an example:

>**Sample 1:** *"Stop doing that! I don't like it when you do that."*

This sample is way too vague, and kids are amazing at playing dumb. I guarantee that giving commands or corrections in this way will only lead to frustration for everyone involved. In contrast, try giving your directives like this:

>**Sample 2:** *"Stop yelling, please. I don't like it when you yell. Speak to me calmly and quietly so that I can understand you."*

In Sample 2, you are stating the behavior you want to see stopped (*yelling*), and you are being specific with the behavior you want to see it replaced with (*speaking calmly and quietly*). This sample leaves no room for arguing and no room to play dumb. The child knows exactly what you want to see stopped and what you want to see instead.

6. Label the behavior, not the child

It is common for parents to say something such as, "*Stop doing that. You are being a bad boy!*" This is an example of labeling the child because you are calling the child a *bad boy*. When doing this, you are making a statement about your child's character. We want to avoid doing that as much as possible. Hearing statements like the one above can contribute to a poor self-esteem over the course of time.

A better way to tackle this might be saying something like, "*Stop yelling. Yelling is not the best choice.*" In this example, you are highlighting that the behavior is the problem, not the child. You are also being specific with the behavior you want to see stopped (*yelling*).

7. Highlight "choice" whenever possible and appropriate

The power of *choice* can be important in parenting. From the toddler years and on, children appreciate the ability to make their own choices, which helps them to develop independence. It is clearly important to provide our children with choices, but only when appropriate. When it comes to discipline, *choice* has a role to play as well.

As mentioned previously in this chapter, semantics and word-choice are powerful in parenting. Let's take another look at the examples given above:

> "*Stop yelling. Yelling is not the best choice.*"

In this example, not only are we being *specific* and avoiding an attack on our child's character, but we are also highlighting *choice*. We are implying to our child that their behavior is a choice. If the behavior is a choice, then the child has the power, capacity, and capability to make a *different* choice. This is empowering to your child, highlights the control that they have over their own behavior, and helps to instill ownership and accountability in our children.

8. When giving directives, use the 4 W's

Try to include the 4 W's into your directives: Who, What, Where, and When. Here is an example of a good, clear directive:

> "Tommy, in 5 minutes, I need you to put on your shoes by the front door."

In this example, Tommy (*The Who*) has been given one directive (*The What:* put on shoes) with a clear expectation of when (*The When:* in 5 minutes) and where (*The Where:* the front door) the task should be done. This directive is clear with the 4 W's of the situation. Although Tommy may not follow through with this directive perfectly, the likelihood of the directive being followed through in the manner expected by the parent is greatly increased.

Practicing efficient and clear communication will improve how well your child responds and complies with your requests and directives. You will see an improvement in behavior from your child and a reduction in frustration and irritability because your child clearly understands what is expected from him. Furthermore, they know what they can do to improve their behavior. This increases the chance that they will meet your expectations in the future.

Parental Warmth & Affection

As a parent, you need to be firm, warm, and affectionate. In this section, we are going to look at how warmth and affection are used in disciplinary sessions. In chapter 4, we discussed the Parent-Child Relationship and its importance in happy and emotionally healthy families. In many ways, the Parent-Child Relationship is intimately intertwined with a wholistic disciplinary approach. As such, you might find that information discussed in chapter 4 and in this section will be similar. The purpose of reviewing this information is to help you better understand how the Parent-Child Relationship has a role in disciplinary sessions and vice versa. With that said, let's look at how you can use warmth and affection in our wholistic disciplinary approach.

Praise

It is a known fact that children want to please their parents, and they crave the attention of their primary caregivers. If children can't gain attention from their parents by behaving in positive ways, they will purposefully engage in negative behaviors. Children would much rather have negative attention from you than no attention at all! This boggles most parents who I work with, and perhaps seems counter-intuitive to you now.

Have you ever noticed that when your child is behaving appropriately, keeping himself entertained, you may not interact with him at all? Perhaps you wash dishes, fold laundry, or accomplish other ordinary tasks. Yet, when your child is misbehaving, you will drop everything that you are doing to address the problem. This is an example of where children will often get more attention from us for misbehaving than they do for behaving appropriately. This creates a dynamic where a child, in order to gain our attention, will purposefully engage in behavior that they know will get them in trouble because they know it will gain our attention.

So, I'll repeat this important concept once more: *children would rather have negative attention from us than no attention at all.* This dynamic begins early on in infancy when we leave babies alone in a swing or playing with toys while we try to accomplish household tasks (or just take a much-needed break!). You aren't being negligent, and this is certainly not the mark of a bad parent, but it does set us up for the dynamic described above. The question then becomes, how can we correct this situation? How can we utilize this same dynamic to encourage positive behavior? The answer is... *praise* often!

Praise is a type of reward that we give our children for a job well done. When your child brings home good grades from school, you praise them, right? If they did a great job in a soccer game, you praise them, correct? It is a reward, and is often the *best* reward you can give your child.

Praising often will create a dynamic where children feel good about themselves, and they will want to continue to feel that way. They also see that they gain your favor and attention. As such, they will want to behave appropriately more often in order to gain more attention (*Sound familiar?*). Essentially, the more you focus on good behavior, the more often good behavior will happen. It's that easy!

Despite the simplicity of this concept, it is probably one of the most difficult ones to follow through with. As parents, we are often overwhelmed with the demands of everyday life. We are all guilty of racing from one task to the next without stopping to think about what our children need from us. As such, we set up the dynamic described above, where we go from task to task and pay little attention to when our children are behaving well and appropriately. It takes hard work to develop a habit of recognizing your child when they are behaving well.

The good news is, all praise is good! Whatever you can muster is going to help you. Like many other concepts in this chapter, however, there are tips that you can follow to improve and maximize the effectiveness of your praise. Take a look at the following tips:

1. Praise specific behaviors

Just like with communication, the more specific, the better! By being specific on what behavior you are praising, your child will have a better understanding of what to do again in the future. For example, saying "*I love how gently you played with the baby*" is more informative for your child than "*Good job!*" Another example might be, "*Thank you for listening to Mommy the first time*

I asked you." This praise is better than, *"Thank you for listening,"* because you are highlighting that you appreciate being listened to the first time as opposed to the 10th.

2. Be sincere and enthusiastic in your praise

Non-verbal communication, such as smiling, thumbs up, and high fives are a nice added touch to your praise, especially for young children. Don't let your teen fool you, however. They might roll their eyes at your thumbs-up, but they secretly enjoy your enthusiasm for their accomplishment.

3. Avoid criticism when praising

Many of us are guilty of this. Have you ever said something like, *"Great job on your homework! Why can't you do it like this all the time?"* This is called a *back-handed compliment.* Has anyone ever complimented you in this way? It doesn't feel sincere, and the critique at the end can cancel out the praise. Here's another example, *"You look nice today. Why can't you always dress this nice?"* Ouch! Say this one to your teen daughter, and you'll probably end up with a door slammed in your face. Stick with the compliment and then bite your tongue after!

4. Praise immediately following behavior

Do your best to reward your child with your praise as soon as you catch them in the act. This helps to ensure that your child is connecting the praise with the behavior that you are trying to increase. If you can't catch them in the act, praise as soon as you are able. Just be sure to explain to your child what they are being praised for. Be as specific as you can!

Remember that *praise* is a type of reward. Use it frequently! Not only does it help increase those behaviors you want to see, but it also helps develop a positive Parent-Child Relationship. You'll be depositing funds into that Emotional Piggy Bank we discussed in chapter 4, and the best part is it's FREE! So, layer on the praise!

Structure of Disciplinary Sessions

I spent much time considering whether or not I would provide specific disciplinary techniques in this book, such as time-outs, removal of privileges, etc. In the end, I decided that diving into specific parenting strategies would retract from the primary purpose of this text: to teach you foundational parenting skills that you could apply throughout your child's lifespan. As such, I shied away from providing you with specific discipline techniques. Instead, we will focus on the structure of disciplinary sessions. You will find this last part will encompass everything we have discussed so far in this section of the chapter. It all comes together, which is why this part is last.

When you have determined a need to discipline your child, you have begun a **disciplinary session**. It includes how you approach your child, what you say to them, and what consequences you administer. In short, it is the actual process of disciplining your child from start to finish. Regardless of what disciplinary technique you use, the effectiveness of your discipline is largely determined by *how* you implement it. Keeping in mind everything we've discussed in this chapter so far, we are going to break the disciplinary session into 3 parts:

1. Presentation
2. Implementation
3. The Wrap-Up

You're going to see how, by combining everything you've learned so far, you can accomplish effective discipline without shame, all while improving your Parent-Child Relationship by establishing mutual respect between you and your child.

Presentation

How you enter a disciplinary session is really going to set the tone for how the whole session is going to turn out. If you enter the disciplinary session with anger, frustration, resentment, etc., your child is going to sense that. Remember our discussion on Conscientious Parenting vs Reactive Parenting? This is where that comes into play. You must be in control of your emotions. If you come into the disciplinary session from a reactive place, you will trigger an immediate emotional response from your child before you ever even start talking. This response may be shame, guilt, anger, or defiance.

Coming into the disciplinary session in a calm manner is going to be a critical first step. If you can manage compassion, this will greatly add a soothing effect to the disciplinary session. You also want to remain firm. Being firm is going to send the message to your child that the situation is serious and you aren't playing games. Finally, enter into the session with the mindset that this is a teachable moment. This will help keep down the sense of guilt or shame your child might begin to feel. Express to your child that you are there to teach them alternate behaviors that are going to get them better results.

Implementation

Implementation is all about how you conduct the disciplinary session. It's essentially the "lecture" portion of your chosen disciplinary method. Ideally, you are going to wait until your child has calmed down enough that they are able to listen. When your child is in the height of a temper tantrum, that's not the time to lecture. In this situation, you're going to want to wait until he has settled down and can focus on you. This is, generally, when sending your child to a quiet space or separating them from the situation that is causing them distress is a good idea. Remember, though, that when you remove them from the space, you should be doing this in a calm manner (i.e. *Presentation*).

During the implementation portion of your session, you'll want to remember all of those tips we learned when we discussed *efficient communication*. This is when your communication skills are put to the test, as well as your ability to remain *conscientious* in your word-choice and in your consequences. Know *what* you are saying and *why* you are saying it. Stay in control of yourself and do your best to not become reactive.

Once your child is calm enough, you should begin the lecture portion of the disciplinary session. Now, when I say "lecture," I don't mean that you talk at your kids. You should be trying to engage them in a dialogue where they can explain to you their side of the story, their own emotions, and express their thought processes. This is important. It shows your child that you care about their opinions and "their side" of the story (particularly important with pre-teens and teens). Be patient as you listen, reflect what you hear often, and truly try to understand the situation from their perspective.

During this dialogue, be sure that you are helping your child to identify their emotions (*"Sounds like you were pretty angry at your brother"*), and help your child to understand how their behavior has affected other people (*"When you yelled at your brother, I think he might have felt embarrassed,"*). Doing this helps to develop empathy, compassion for others, and grows your child's emotional maturity. Remember to present these emotions in a calm way to help encourage the dialogue and keep down any potential feelings of shame or resentment or picking sides.

Finally, be specific when discussing the behavior you disapprove of, and be specific in what you would like to see next time. Encourage your child to think of alternative behaviors that they can try with you. This is a great practice because you are modeling problem-solving skills to them, as well as critical thinking. For younger kids, you'll need to provide these alternative behaviors to them.

The Wrap-Up

It is important for us to remember that kids are always going to make mistakes. They are new to this world, and their ability to assess the consequences of their behaviors is not fully developed. After all, even as adults, we *still* make mistakes. Don't we all deserve a little grace then?

When ending our disciplinary sessions, we should remain calm and firm, but also display empathy, warmth, and affection. Being able to display these emotions and behaviors goes back to modeling, whereby showing yourself as being calm, firm, and empathetic helps your child to learn and reflect the same behaviors back to you during times of stress. Being calm, firm, and empathetic also models graciousness, and will allow your children to actually *listen* to you because they aren't zeroing in on the volume or tone of your voice.

Finally, when ending the disciplinary session, always end with an *Act of Love*. All kids want to know that, even though they have displeased you or have hurt someone in their family, they are still loved. It is very important to make sure that your child feels loved and accepted by you, regardless of their behavior. One way to accomplish this is by ending the disciplinary session with an Act of Love, such as a hug or a kiss from you. Let your child know that, no matter what, you will always love them! I cannot emphasize the importance of this enough. This helps to reaffirm for your child that they are still loved, wanted, and accepted by you regardless of the mistakes that they may have made. This is the *Parental Warmth & Affection* component at its best, and it helps to repair any minor damage caused to the Parent-Child relationship by the disciplinary session. When disciplining siblings, you can encourage them to give each other a hug, shake hands, or anything else that would help to display love towards one another. This powerful act helps to reaffirm to your child that they are inherently "good" (something we discussed in our Parenting Philosophy section) and worthy of love.

This helps to further emphasize that the behavior is the problem, not the child.

9.3 Final Thoughts on Discipline

I hope that this detailed and thorough look at discipline has been helpful. We started off broad by looking at your overall home environment and then honed it down to you. We discussed tips for more effective discipline, tips for better communication, and broke down the disciplinary session into 3 parts. Hopefully you can see how everything has come together and has formed a cohesive picture.

Now, I know some individuals will be disappointed that I didn't address specific parenting techniques in this chapter or discuss other related topics such as managing power struggles. The reality is, there are hundreds of books that do a wonderful job of tackling these topics. If you feel, however, that you want my specific spin on these concepts, you can check out my website at: kcdreisbach.com. My blog covers all of it! Not only will you find some of the items discussed in this book, but you'll find help on more nuanced items such as:

- How to manage power struggles
- How to manage anger outbursts and temper tantrums
- How to get your kids to listen the first time you ask
- How to manage sibling rivalries

That's just a taste of what you can find there. There is so much more! So, forgive me for not diving deep into specific parenting techniques, but please help yourself to the abundance of parenting articles on my blog.

10

Co-Parenting

10.1 Who or What are Co-Parents?

Pretty much every family has a co-parent. For a single mom, the co-parent might be her chosen caregivers or a daycare worker. For a couple who is raising their children together, they both are co-parents. For me, my co-parents are my husband and my own parents. Every family is different. A co-parent is essentially anyone who is parenting your child for a large portion of the time.

These people, due to how much time they spend raising your child, are also responsible for the outcome! They are contributing to who your child becomes in adulthood. Your co-parents are invested in your child whether the investment is emotional (such as a grandparent), biological (such as the birth mother or father), marital (as in stepparents), or fiscal (as in daycare workers). It doesn't matter how; these people are invested. And, because they spend so much time with your child, they are contributing to the emotional, moral, and behavioral development of the child.

Co-parenting is a pretty tricky topic. In an ideal co-parenting situation, the co-parents share common/similar views on everything. They share the same household rules, the same discipline style, the same rewards, the same values, same morals and ethics, and the same life lessons, etc. Essentially, that co-parent is an extension of you! This, however, is rarely the reality. The reality is far messier and a lot trickier to manage.

10.2 The Realities of Co-Parenting

In most co-parenting situations, no one agrees on everything. It is a messy process, frustrating, and totally normal. Most parents find themselves constantly arguing and bickering between themselves and their co-parents. In my own house, my kids are not allowed to jump on the sofa. When we go to the homes of other people, I instruct them that they are not allowed to jump on the sofa, even if the other kids in the home do so. When my children go to their grandma's house for the day, it is not uncommon for me to come and find them jumping on the sofa. When I scold them and instruct them to get down, Grandma will typically come in and tell me, it's "okay" because she gave them permission. This is an example of the realities of co-parenting. Now, in my situation it's not too big of a deal because this grandparent doesn't care for the children very often. If she were to watch the children daily or multiple times a week, however, it would become very important for her and I to agree on the parenting rules we would be using with my kids.

Divorced parents frequently have to face the nightmares of co-parenting. I had a friend who had divorced her husband some years ago, and they had two children together. The boys lived with her Monday through Friday and would visit their father on the weekends. My friend is great mom. She had rules that she enforced consistently and was a very loving mother. Her ex-husband was also very loving, but not very good at following the household rules. So, when kids went to his home to visit, they were allowed to run amok. They would stay up late, eat junk food every day, and never did their homework. When they would come home, my friend used to say it was like raising wolves every Monday. She would have to go back to reminding them about the rules of the house, re-establish appropriate bedtimes, and so on. For a long time, the kids thought she was the "Mean Mommy," and he was the "Fun Daddy." This is just another example that demonstrates what some of the difficulties are with co-parenting.

The truth is that co-parenting is either going to bring you together or it is going to create dissension between you and your co-parents. If you experience dissension, then your co-parenting relationship becomes vulnerable to triangulation and parental sabotage.

Triangulation

Triangulation is a theory first formulated by Murray Bowen and his approach to family therapy, which is known as *family systems therapy.* Bowen believed most relationships involved one or more third parties. Essentially, everyone was shadowed, in some way, by a third person. He theorized that as tension grew between two people, the anxiety that would develop would become too much to handle. As such, the two people in the relationship would reach out, subconsciously, to a third person to help stabilize the relationship (Good Therapy, *Triangulation*). Over time, this process becomes fixed and becomes the norm for that relationship. This is common in co-parenting relationships and children. Furthermore, triangles form a rich breeding ground for future problems between the co-parents.

To better understand, let's look at an example. When I was a kid, my mom and dad used to argue all of the time. There had been some conflict in their relationship, and they just never seemed to get over it. Instead of facing each other, and managing this conflict, they turned outward to a third person in order to vent and let off steam. My dad and my mom, would both, frequently come to me and complain about the other parent. I would listen and offer advice as best as I could. When I was younger, it was difficult to be privy to so much information about their relationship. As I got older, it wasn't a problem. When I moved out of the house, they began to vent to my little sister who still lived in the home. When she moved out of the house, the arguments between the two of them increased and became overwhelming for everyone involved. It could be said that the relationship almost fell apart. They were able to pull through. The question: Why is it that their children moving out of the home caused the relationship to almost fall apart?

In this example, the strain in the marriage had become too unbearable for both my parents to manage. As such, they drew in a third person to help stabilize the marriage by utilizing the third person to vent and let off steam. This third person was me. This is a triangle. When I left the home, it meant that the third person (i.e. *me*) was no longer there and the couple needed someone else to help stabilize the triangle. As such, they triangulated my sister. When she left the home, there was no one left to triangulate. Therefore, the couple was forced to face each other for the first time. In the book, *Family Therapy: Concepts and Methods*, Michael Nichols explains the reason why triangles are problematic is because they become habitual. In doing so, they corrupt and distort the original relationship. He further explains that, although triangles can help ease tension, they don't allow the conflict to resolve, which causes the root problem to remain and the relationship to potentially deteriorate over time (116).

Parental Sabotage

Parental sabotage is my own name for when someone undermines your parenting. This can be a huge problem, because it teaches your child that what you have to say, isn't necessarily what the child has to do. This is really common with parents and grandparents or with parents and their ex's. A good example of this might be if your child comes to you and asks if they can buy something from the toy store. You say "no," but then Grandma comes over and buys them something anyways. Although Grandma may mean well, and just wants to spoil your child, it is no help to you because all she has done is undermined your parenting. By Grandma saying she will buy the child a toy after you said "no," she is demonstrating to the child that she has more power than you when it comes to the child. This creates larger issues later, when Grandma is not around, and you have to try to parent this child. The child will not see you as having authority.

Parental sabotage is frequently a subconscious process that occurs without meaning to. Grandparents, for example, do not intentionally mean to undermine your parenting (at least not usually), but are likely to do it often. Your spouse may not intentionally undermine your parenting either, but may do it because they don't agree with your parenting style or chosen technique. This is the reality of co-parenting.

Triangulation and parental sabotage cause all kinds of issues when it comes to parenting your kids. You may see your child becoming manipulative, may be confused about what the rules actually are, or they may begin to display disruptive behaviors.

10.3 Preventing Co-Parenting Disasters

Now that we know about all the different problems you can face with co-parenting, let's talk about how you can prevent these co-parenting disasters. In my opinion, the easiest is to start early on during pregnancy. You should be discussing different aspects of parenting, such as parenting philosophies that you both share or disagree on, discipline techniques, and reward systems, among other topics. You may also want to discuss items such as how to deal with grandparents, or other people in your family who may be around your children frequently.

When I was pregnant with our first daughter, my husband and I would frequently talk about parenting. If we were in a store and we saw a situation occur between a child and a parent or between a child and his sibling, we would take the opportunity to point it out to one another and then discuss it. We would discuss what we would or would not do in a similar situation. We did this all the time: in restaurants, at parties, in movie theaters, and so forth. The results, however, were my husband and I had a fairly good idea about how we wanted to parent our future child. Moreover, we continue to do this to this very day.

I highly encourage you and your co-parent do the same thing. As your child grows you should continue to have these discussions with one another in a very open and candid manner. If your child is 18, it is never too late to start. I will warn you that this is not the only answer to solving all of your co-parenting problems. I can say, however, that this process will help in reducing the amount of arguments you and your co-partner will have later on.

It is also helpful to mention that you should always remember what your default parenting style is. You should also make a note of what your co-parent's default parenting style is. Remember that your parenting style will affect how you manage situations under stress or when you are pinned in a corner. The same is true for your co-parent(s). Don't discipline when under stress or angry, and don't feel forced into giving answers or responses when you haven't had the opportunity to think about the situation. It is okay to say, *"I have to think about it with Mommy,"* or, *"I need to talk about this with Daddy first."*

Next, don't disagree in front of your children. The worst thing you can do when it comes to co-parenting, is to disagree with your co-parent in front of the kids. This is parental sabotage in action and it undermines your co-parent's parenting. You should always have discussions about these types of disagreements in private, behind closed doors. If you can't find a place without the kids, then find another way to communicate. I don't care if you speak in Pig Latin, or you use smoke signals, or you come up with secret phrases and code words. Just don't undermine your partner's parenting in front of the kids.

You should both be treating each other with respect in front of the kids and also be treating your children with respect. If you find that you are having a lot of difficulty with your co-parent, then you should consider seeking an objective opinion, such as a family therapist, who can listen to you and your partner discuss the matter and potentially shed some clarity on the situation. Consider compromises if you have disagreements with how to approach a parenting problem. If all else fails, then agree to disagree and pick a boss. In therapy, it is common for me to encounter parents who can't agree on how to manage a parenting situation. As such, one of the recommendations I have given parents is for them to pick a boss. This means to pick the parent who is going to be responsible for delegating rewards and consequences. Typically, when I suggest this, the parent who was causing most of the issues gets on board and decides he's willing to compromise.

11

Parenting & Marriage

I think everyone can agree that so much affects your parenting, but parenting also really affects your marriage! Your relationship with your significant other completely changes the minute you bring home a baby and you begin the journey of raising a child together. Now, when I say "marriage" I want you to understand that I'm talking about couples in a serious relationship who are raising a child together. I don't necessarily mean "marriage" in the classical sense of the word. For this chapter, when you read the word "marriage," just know that I'm talking about two people in a committed relationship.

There are several ways that parenting affects your marriage. First off, it can cause dissension due to different parenting styles or ideas. This dissension can lead to frequent arguments, bitterness and stress on the relationship. Second, the focus shifts from the couple to the children. As such, the couple begins to forget to nourish their own relationship because they're so busy nourishing the relationship with their children. Intimacy decreases and private moments between co-parents all but disappear. Lastly, this increases irritability between the couple and slowly changes the marital narrative. In previous chapters, we've discussed the importance of the family narrative. In this chapter, we will discuss the importance of the love narrative (i.e. marital narrative). We will go through each one of these issues that can arise in the marital relationship once kids are brought on board, and then we will tackle rebuilding the marriage.

11.1 Dissension in the Relationship

Dissension is a pretty fancy word to describe arguing. As already mentioned, adding kids into a romantic relationship can increase disagreements between the people in that relationship. These disagreements can arise over anything, including parenting styles, disciplinary techniques, how to manage caregivers, where to put the child in school, etc. Overtime, arguments take over the relationship. The more you argue, the more the story of the relationship changes, which we will discuss a little bit later. What we will discuss right now is what arguments can do to that relationship itself and the people in the relationship. Dissension and frequent arguing can leave behind bitterness, especially if you feel like you're doing all of the work in the relationship.

Have you ever felt this way? Have you ever felt like you come home, make dinner, take care of the kids, prepare lunches for the following day, do dishes, and so on, only to look over and find your partner sitting on the sofa enjoying a drink and watching their favorite TV show? Many people find themselves in this position and find themselves feeling really angry with their partner. They feel as though they are the one doing all of the work.

I remember one day coming home from work and feeling completely overwhelmed with all of the tasks I had to complete once I came home. From cooking and bathing the kids to cleaning and preparing for the next day, I was stressed and looking for an argument. My husband made it all too easy, since he was watching TV with his feet up the entire time that I was busily working. As you can imagine, we had an argument about how I felt I was doing all of the work. Although there was validity behind my feelings, the bitterness was making it difficult for me to step back and look at all the hard work he *also* did such as working two jobs, doing all of the handyman repair on the weekends, among other things. At that moment, I was unable to think clearly and remember all of the work he did. This is an example of how bitterness can grow in a relationship once kids are in the mix. This then drives a wedge in the relationship which may lead to several other issues such as triangulation, behavior issues with the kids, mental health issues for the parents, etc.

I want to take a moment to tell a quick story about a real client who I worked with. Her name was Nancy and she was living with her boyfriend, who was the father of her child. Nancy and her boyfriend had been together for quite some time and their son was about 2 years old when she came in to see me in therapy. She came in because she was suffering from depression, felt alone in life, unsatisfied, and always felt sad, hopeless, and helpless.

As I worked with Nancy in therapy, she began to make significant improvements with her diagnosis, but something always happened that would cause her to spiral back into her depression. This turned out to be her boyfriend. What I quickly discovered was happening, was that as Nancy's symptoms would improve, she would go home, her and her boyfriend would get into some sort of argument over raising their son, and she would then spiral back into her depressive state. It quickly became obvious that the relationship between her and her boyfriend was causing her depression.

Once I noticed this connection, I requested that her boyfriend attend therapy with her. Once I brought him into the treatment room with Nancy, I was able to begin working on their relationship and how they managed the stress from raising their son. As I relieved the stress and helped them rebuild their relationship, arguments became less frequent between Nancy and her boyfriend, and her depressive symptoms lessened. Eventually, Nancy was able to successfully leave treatment.

Nancy's relationship with her boyfriend turned upside down when her child came into the picture. Although they both cared greatly for their son, they struggled on how to parent him because they had such differing parenting styles. Going unchecked, these frequent arguments about how to parent their son increased the strain on the relationship. This caused Nancy to develop a mental health condition. Once I was able to piece this information together for Nancy, treatment was quick, fast, and easy.

11.2 Shifting Focus to the Kids

When we have kids, so much of our life becomes them, and we forget to nurture the relationship we have with our partner. Have you ever had a friend you used to hang out with all the time? Then one of you moved away, and you slowly became strangers overtime? It's because you weren't able to effectively nourish the relationship! Our relationship with our spouse is no different. So many couples become strangers to one another because they forget to continuously learn who their partner is. Think of it this way, are you the same person who you were one year ago? What about 3 years ago? What about 5 or 10 years ago? Chances are you are a very different person and so are they.

If you changed, you can bet they changed too! It's silly of us to think that our partners remain exactly the same, but they aren't. Everyone changes, whether because of life experiences, a job change, new friends, death, etc., all of these events guarantee changes in your partner. Sometimes, the changes might be small, and others might be big, but compound those changes over the course of years and you can bet that the person you married years ago is not the same person today. When a relationship only has two people, it's a lot easier to keep up on who your partner is. This is typically because you spend most of your time together, go out frequently, and get to discuss who you are to one another weekly. When children come into the picture, however, your time shifts and so does your attention. You become hyper focused on the needs, wants, and all the changes that child is going through daily. With so much of your time, energy, and focus on the child, it is easy to see how you lose focus on your partner.

Kids also make it difficult for couples to engage in intimate moments. With a new baby, a snoopy toddler, or an anxious teenager, sex practically disappears. Body changes from pregnancy, weight gain from poor nutrition and lack of exercise, and a more hectic life can cause reduced confidence, especially for women. Stress and exhaustion tend to decrease libido creating an end result of little or no sex in the relationship. This is simply another way that couples begin to lose sight of one another. Pair the lack of intimacy with the lack of nourishment in the relationship and you can understand why your spouse slowly becomes a stranger to you right before your eyes.

11.3 Change in the Marital Narrative

The last one to discuss is the change in the marital narrative. This one is closely tied to our first point discussed (i.e. dissension between both persons in the relationship). As stress increases, intimacy decreases, and more arguments arise between the couple. Both individuals become more irritable with one another, which slowly changes the narrative. Another way to think of the narrative is the story of the couple.

In order to better understand this concept, I want you to think about a couple of different pairs of glasses. We've all tried on sunglasses before, and we know that there are different types of lenses. Some lenses are dark in color, others are amber, and some are even a rosy shade. If you put the dark colored lenses on, the world has a hint of grey to it and seems darker in nature. If you swap the glasses out for the amber colored ones, the world now obtains a brown shade. Finally, if you switch out those glasses for the rose-colored ones, you will find that the world has a pinkish tint to it. The color of the glasses is like your mood, and how your mood affects the way you see the world.

When you are in a good mood, you are more likely to view different situations in a positive light and are less likely to become annoyed or irritable with troublesome situations. If you are in a bad mood, you will see the world in a more negative light. You are more likely to become upset and angry over the smallest mishap. The lesson here is that mood oftentimes affect how we view situations in our daily lives. So, as you become more stressed, irritable, and/or overwhelmed, the more likely it is that you'll be bitter with your spouse. This, in turn, slowly changes the narrative of the relationship. You will see situations with your spouse in a negative light and be less likely to see the positives of any given situation with your spouse. In doing this, the memories that you will have of your spouse take on a more negative quality. The more negative memories you have, the more likely that the story of your relationship becomes a negative one.

11.4 Rebuilding the Marriage... with Kids!

Understanding the different, subtle ways that having kids can wreak havoc on your marriage is important. It is also important to know, however, that having kids does not mean that your marriage is doomed. It is possible to have children with whom you have a dedicated relationship with, and also have a loving, positive relationship with your spouse. So, now the time has come for us to get our act together and begin reconnecting with our spouse, all while having kids.

In this section I'm going to give you a few different ways that you can begin working on your marital relationship today, improving and nourishing the relationship. The key to rebuilding your marriage is rebuilding the marital narrative. If you recall, in previous chapters we discussed ways to improve the Parent-Child relationship. One of those ways was by improving the family narrative. Your marital relationship is no different. It should come as no surprise that the key to improving your marriage is by having a rich and positive marital narrative. Furthermore, there are several ways that you can go about improving your marital narrative. Remember that you have an Emotional Piggy Bank with your spouse. The more you argue with your spouse, for whatever the reason, the more you withdraw funds from the emotional bank account. The less time you spend with your spouse in building the relationship, such as sharing intimate moments, the less you deposit into the account. This is why the relationship begins to fade. So, once again, the key is to begin depositing more funds into the account than you withdraw. But how do you go about doing that when you're already so busy?

Go on a Date Night

Having regularly scheduled date nights is a great way to help deposit more funds into your bank account. This can be tricky, however, because you have to be able to find someone to watch the kids. Consider finding a nanny/babysitter who you can hire periodically so that you can have a night off. You can also talk to relatives or family members to see if they can babysit for you. The point is to try and get some time together and separate from the kids so that you can nourish the relationship. This doesn't have to be weekly, but if you can manage this on a weekly basis then more power to you! The key is to simply try to squeeze in some date time. If you're low on funds, then enjoy a night in with a candlelit dinner on your own dinner table with your favorite movie. This works just as well as going out to a restaurant and checking out the latest blockbuster at the theater.

Be Intimate

Don't forget that intimacy is important in relationships, but it doesn't have to always be about sex! Take time to hug one another when you come home from work, kiss one another in passing, or have a few minutes of cuddle time on the sofa before you have to put the kids to bed. The point is to remain in some sort of physical contact frequently. You don't always have to be looking for an opportunity to take off your clothes, but enjoying physical touch is good for the relationship too. Simple caresses, hugs, and cuddles can go a long way in helping a couple to feel physically connected and intimate with one another. So, start giving some hugs, and start stealing some kisses!

Get to Know One Another... Continuously!

Remember how earlier in this chapter I talked about how people change? One of the best ways to help rebuild your relationship is to continuously get to know your partner. John Gottman is frequently touted as one of the best couple's therapists of our time, and his research has changed the way marital problems are managed in the therapy room. Gottman developed a concept he called **Love Maps**, which is all of the relevant information you know about your partner that you have stored in your brain (48). His research found that couples who have great knowledge about their partners (i.e. detailed love maps) are much better at coping with stressful life events. In his book, he shared that one of largest causes of marital dissatisfaction and divorce is children. When couples have that first baby, the relationship takes a hard hit. His research noted that marital relationships that thrived after the birth of a child had detailed love maps before the child was ever born; whereas marriages that failed to have these love maps often deteriorated and were lost over time (49). Love maps serve as a protective factor for marriages, especially when facing challenging or strenuous times.

When was the last time that you asked your partner what their favorite movie was? Chances are, it was probably on one of your first dates! But can you even begin to count how many movies you have seen since then? Do you know how many other films have come out since then? There's a chance that your spouse may have a new favorite movie, and you don't even know it! Once again, if you have changed, then so has your spouse. Take some time and get to know them all over again.

The other day, I went on a date with my husband. I took my own advice and asked him some basic questions that I thought I already knew the answer to. I asked him what his favorite food was, which I had always known to be pizza. He surprised me by saying that he really doesn't have a favorite food, but that a good New York steak was one of his favorites. When I realized that I didn't know that simple, basic question, I went ahead and asked others, such as, what is your favorite restaurant? He then took the lead and began to ask me the same questions back. We got to know each other all over again, and it was a very nice experience.

Find Shared Experiences

So many couples say that they don't have anything to talk about. As such, they end up talking only about the kids. The time has come to think of some new conversation topics. If after getting to know your partner over again you find yourselves stuck, then start sharing something new together. Something my husband and I do is share a show together. At one time it was *Army Wives*, *Lost*, and then *Bones*. We would watch the shows together after the kids went to bed. This allowed us to have something that we could talk about that had nothing to do with the kids. Some couples like to do this with books, and will read books together and discuss these topics when they go on their date nights. One couple I worked with would read Bible verses together and then debate them on date nights. The point is to develop conversations that are about both of you when you are together. The point is to engage in more shared experiences other than just raising your kids. When you were dating, you experiences many new things together such as new restaurants, movies, hiking trails, beach trips, etc. Once you have kids, many of these experiences new include your children. There's noting wrong with this! It is nice, however, to have some experiences that are just for you and your spouse, a hearkening back to those dating days. So, what experiences can you share together on a regular basis? How you want to master this is up to you, but get started and have fun doing it.

Try to Focus on the Positive

Just like we should focus as much as possible on what our kids do right, we need to do the same with our spouse. This doesn't mean that we forget or forgive the errors the other person makes, but rather, we should choose our battles wisely, and keep it to things that are most important. After that, we should see the good our partner is capable of. Just like children react better to positive parenting techniques, so do our spouses. Most people want to be rewarded, not get in trouble. As such, highlighting the things that your spouse is doing correctly, acknowledging those things, and praising them for those things can actually help our spouse in doing those things more frequently. It also helps to maintain a more positive marital relationship and view of the other person. Once again, this doesn't mean that you ignore important issues that need to be discussed. By all means, make sure you have those battles because they are important, but *do* pick and choose your battles to that which is essential and non-negotiable for you.

In the same vein, we need to remember that our partners have positive qualities too, no matter how mad at them we might be. It's important to remember these things when we feel our frustrations rising. Remembering our partner's positive qualities can help to prevent the death of the relationship, even if you are actively trying to deal with some of their flaws (Gottman and Silver 65). Keeping focused on the positive qualities of your spouse can help maintain a happy marital narrative, which in turn, helps to keep your marriage from falling into a place of contempt. As Gottman and Silver share, the antidote to contempt and hate are admiration and love (65).

Be Gracious and Be Grateful

Gratitude and graciousness are an important aspect when we look at building up relationships. Too often in therapy, I hear people say that their spouses forget about them or never think to acknowledge them in some way. I tend to challenge my clients on this idea by asking them is it really that their spouse forgot about them or is it that *they* created the situation by lacking gratitude. I can't tell you how many people, initially, get a little rise out of this idea from me. But I want you to think about this before you discard it.

When someone does something nice for you, how many times do you find yourself saying, "You shouldn't have," "That's too kind of you," "I don't deserve this," or "I feel so bad that you bought this for me." My guess is that you've probably said this a few times, and if you're like me, you probably say it almost always when someone does something nice for you. The problem with this is that it takes away the joy that someone gets from giving you something. Take a second and think about when you give a gift to someone you love. Doesn't it feel good to give that gift to that person? Aren't you excited to see how they're going to react when they see the gift you bought them? Now, what does it feel like when that person looks at you and says, "I feel bad that you bought this for me," "You spent too much money," or "I really wish you wouldn't have." Although you still feel joy in giving a gift to the person, it's not quite the same. There's a part of you that feels you have to try to convince the other person it's okay you bought this gift for them.

Graciousness and gratitude allow the other person to know that you truly appreciate what they got for you while suppressing the urge to tell people that you are somehow undeserving of what they have done for you. You need to remember that, just like you enjoy making others happy, your spouse likes doing the same thing for you! I encourage you to try a new approach. Try saying:

- Thank you
- I really appreciate that you did this for me
- It's so thoughtful that you did this
- I'm so happy
- I really feel special when you do this for me

Graciousness and gratefulness are forms of that positive reinforcement that we've talked about earlier in this chapter and in previous chapters. By letting the other person know how much you appreciate and enjoy what they have done for you, you are more likely to increase this type of behavior back from them. More importantly, this continues to build and enrich the marital narrative.

Barring situations of domestic violence and abuse, and assuming a regular, normal marital relationship, following these tips will truly help to build up and improve the marital relationship you have now. The best thing is you can begin doing this right now. Today, you can begin creating situations that help foster and enrich your love life with your spouse, all while raising children. For more help on improving your marriage, check out the following books:

- *The Seven Principles for Making Marriage Work* by John Gottman and Nan Silver
- *The Relationship Cure* by John Gottman and Joan DeClaire
- *10 Lessons to Transform Your Marriage* by John Gottman, Julie Schwartz, and Joan DeClaire

In our next chapter, we will be moving on to parental burnout and talking about all the different aspects that contribute to parents feeling too overwhelmed and too stressed with their home life. I'll also be tackling how to treat and prevent parental burnout in the future.

12

Managing Parental Burnout

At this point, we have traveled full circle. We've covered the following topics on our journey thus far:

- Understanding Wholistic Parenting
- Discussed parenting philosophies
- Reviewed the Parent-Child relationship
- Gained basic knowledge of the psychosocial development of children
- Understanding how children's emotions play into their behaviors
- Learned how to discipline our children no matter how old they are
- Reviewed how to repair damaged relationships

- Tackled how to manage co-parenting and improving your romantic relationship

We are now moving on to discussing parental burnout. But, what is parental burnout? Stated simply, parental burnout is when you are just tired and done. You're exhausted emotionally and physically and feel as though you have given everything you could possibly give. You find yourself feeling hopeless, helpless, or feeling like the work never ends. That perfect parenting perception that you thought was going to be your life when you had a baby is dead and gone. Parental burnout is real, and it happens to everyone!

12.1 What is Parental Burnout?

When working with women in therapy, especially moms, I frequently need to reassure them that they don't need to feel embarrassed, ashamed, or guilty to admit that they're burned out. I think moms, in particular, are prone to feeling as though they need to be happy all the time, and that everything in their life must be perfect. But parenting is hard work, and the dynamics that are created by having a child in the home greatly impact every aspect of your life. It is only natural that at some point you would begin to feel tired, overwhelmed, and just burned out. In fact, if you think about it, it's almost impossible to not reach a point in your parenting career where you don't feel burnt out. Let's look at all the different reasons why you might be feeling this way.

Poor Eating Habits

As a parent you probably have pretty terrible eating habits. You likely eat cold food most of the time and, if you have a baby or a toddler, end up eating scraps more often than you'd like to admit. Caffeine runs your motor all day long, so you're probably drinking too much coffee. You are probably dehydrated because you aren't drinking enough water (you're too busy looking for your next dose of caffeine), and junk food is your primary source of nutrition because you are snacking on chips or needing to pick up fast food due to the chaoticness of your life. In my case, for a long time, I found myself skipping meals, not because I wasn't hungry, but because I could never find the time to just sit and eat.

Poor Sleep

If you have a young toddler or even a preschooler who sleeps poorly, you probably sleep terribly every night. Your child is continuously getting up in the night to either to go potty, because of bad dreams, or because he's thirsty. This means you are continuously waking up too. This means that your sleep is not nearly as restorative as it should be because it is frequently interrupted. For some parents, stress has their mind going on and on all night long, making it difficult to fall asleep and stay asleep.

Sleep was probably one of the biggest battles I had while raising my older child. She didn't sleep through the night until about 3 years of age, and woke approximately 3 to 5 times every single night. It is safe to say that, for approximately three years, I slept horribly. I was chronically sleep-deprived, leading me to constantly get sick with colds or flus, and making me cranky all of the time. When I got a new job, I found the stress of trying to learn and manage my new job made it difficult for me to fall asleep at night because my mind was constantly running, thinking about all of the tasks I needed to accomplish the next day. Unsurprisingly, I discovered that I am not a great mom when I'm sleep deprived.

Familial Stress

Familial Stress is all of the stressful events, interactions, and experiences that cause you stress within your family and household. As one might suspect, these stressors ware on your emotions and your tolerance. The more your tolerance and emotions are worn, the more likely you are to become irritable and an *Angry Mommy*. Finally, if your child has behavioral issues, or some other type of health issue, you are chronically experiencing high stress levels. Because of this, you are at a high risk for parental burnout

When we look at all of these different components, it is really easy to see how anyone would be burned out at this point! In fact, most people would quit this job by now except that you can't, so what do you do?

12.2 Treating & Preventing Parental Burnout

As the famous sports quote goes, "the key to a good offense is a good defense." The good news for us as parents is that the way to help treat parental burnout is also the same way you help prevent it. This means that if you are already burned out, there are steps that you can take that will help you to feel refreshed and motivated again on your parenting journey. Furthermore, these same steps will help to prevent future burn out. Let's take a look at what these steps are and discuss them in a little more detail.

Caring for Your Body

The most important thing you need to do in order to treat and prevent parental burnout is to take care of your physical body. Always remember that if your body is falling apart, you will not be able to care for your family. As such, you must care for your body first. Without this, everything else will fall apart. When you have a healthy body, you are much more likely to feel happier, more energetic, and just better. So, how can you help care for your body?

Sleep

No matter how you do it, try to make sure you get sleep every day. Take naps if you have to, or sleep in a different room. Do whatever it is you need to do to make sure you get enough sleep. For myself, when I find that I have gone several nights without a good night's rest because the kids have been sick or something else has been bothering me, I sleep in a different room. I let my husband know that I'm going to sleep downstairs in our guest room while he sleeps upstairs with the kids. He manages them so that I can get a good, restorative night's rest. When he's sick, he does the same thing. The person who is sick sleeps downstairs in the guest room to ensure that they get a full, restorative night's rest. This goes a long way in helping us to feel rejuvenated and refreshed.

Make Sure You Eat

As already mentioned, our eating habits as parents tend to be pretty poor. As such, we should work towards improving how we eat, when we eat, and what we eat. The most basic way to nourish your body is to avoid skipping meals. Sometimes that can be pretty hard. Consider purchasing meal replacement shakes, protein bars, and so on to help yourself in making sure that you keep your body nourished. If you're going to snack, try your best to snack healthily. I found that in my house, as long as I keep from buying items like cookies and candy, and stock the pantry with healthier snacks as well as fresh fruit, I either don't snack or snack healthily. The same goes for my kids, who will eat whatever they can find in the pantry. Now, this doesn't mean that you don't enjoy a little piece of cake now and again. It's important to indulge sometimes; you just don't want it to become a daily habit. You may also consider buying supplements to make sure that you're getting all of the nutrition that you need. For example, I found out I was deficient in vitamin D. So, now I take a supplement. Talk to your doctor and make sure that your body has everything it needs.

Maintain Basic Hygiene

Please take your showers! There is nothing so basic as getting a bath into your schedule. Everyone wants to feel clean! But how many of us go several days without showering and then rely on deodorant, body spray, and a messy bun to get us by another day? I'm guilty! Trust me, sacrifice the 5 minutes of extra sleep to squeeze in a shower so that you can still feel like a human being when you're wiping up another poopy butt!

Exercise

Exercise is one of the most powerful things that you can do to help your body stay healthy and help your mind feel healthy. This is so powerful, in fact, that it is one of the keys to treating depression. When you exercise, your body releases endorphins into your brain, and these endorphins help you feel better. You actually feel happy. This has been dubbed by some experts as a "runner's high." As such, I frequently recommend exercise as part of treatment in depression. Many parents, however, feel that they don't have time for exercise, but what they don't realize is that exercise doesn't need to be a trip to the gym. Taking a walk as a family in the afternoon or evening is just as good for you as walking on the treadmill at the gym. My husband and I don't get much time to exercise on our own, but we try to make walking in our neighborhood as a family a common occurrence in our household. It serves as a great bonding activity for us and our kids, and it helps me to gain the exercise that I need to help my body stay strong and feel good.

Caring for Your Mind

Caring for your mind is also a really important aspect of preventing parental burnout. So much of parental burnout is strongly related to your mental health and your emotional well-being. It should be one of your top priorities. In order to help you care for your mind, you should really work on nourishing it in as many different ways as possible. One of these ways would be ensuring that you get enough sleep, as we have already discussed above. But there are many other aspects to nourishing your mind.

Engage in Relaxation

Engaging relaxation is an important component to helping you de-stress and relax. During times of stress, our body releases a hormone called **cortisol,** which is one of the primary hormones that can lead to conditions such as heart disease (Mayo Clinic, *Healthy Lifestyle*). It would make sense that you would want to reduce how often you have cortisol flowing in your body as much as possible. To do this, decompressing and relaxing is a big component to caring for your mind and body. How you decompress is completely up to you. Some ideas might be to read a book that you enjoy before bed, writing in a journal, or writing poetry if that is something that you enjoy. Some individuals like to paint, crochet, or engage in other kinds of crafts. A girlfriend of mine truly enjoys getting massages and facials on a regular basis. If that's too expensive, try a Spa Day at home. This can also be a fun activity to do if you have girls in the home and want to spend some time bonding with them too. As stated, it doesn't matter what you do, as long as you nourish your mind and engage in relaxation as much as possible.

Take a Mental Health Day

A Mental Health Day is something that is common among therapists. Essentially, it's a day that you play hooky from work. In many ways, I think it's important for parents to get to take a Mental Health Day too. For my family, my husband will sometimes ask if he can go off-roading with the forest service every couple of months. This is a Mental Health Day for him, a day where he doesn't have to worry about being a dad or husband; he can just worry about riding a bike and being a guy. I'll have Mental Health Days where I schedule a facial, a massage, or simply go out to lunch by myself, so that I can relax, enjoy a hot meal, and not have to worry about anyone else but me. Taking a Mental Health Day once a month is quite doable for parents, and it can really help in recharging those spent batteries. Give it a try! You might find out that one day off every month takes you where you need to go in terms of relaxation.

Vent with Someone

It's important for adults to have adult conversations, and part of this is getting some time to vent and let off steam. Most folks will lean on their spouse or partner, but sometimes that person is not emotionally available. This is when you need to reach out to a Mom's Group, Postpartum Group, other family members and friends, or a therapist. Therapists are not only for individuals who have a mental health condition like depression. Many individuals find a therapist just because they want to know that every week, there is an hour dedicated just to them and their own needs! Taking care of your Emotional-Self allows for you to have more patience and empathy when your child is testing your limits. This is an important part of great self-care. I think you will find this helps you to feel much better, even if you are still sleep deprived and rocking the messy hair bun.

Engage in Gestures of Self-Love

Most people conceptualize self-care as a 90-minute massage or a trip to the Caribbean. These are incredibly nice, but expensive and short lived. If you do manage that big cruise, once it's over, you are right back where you started. True self-care are those little acts of self-love that you give yourself every day. It's the extra 10-minutes of sleep in the morning, or getting up 15-minutes early so you can enjoy your cup of coffee while it's still hot in a quiet house. Perhaps it's cutting yourself a little slack when you forget something at home, or taking an extra day off of work to enjoy some peace and quiet while the kids go to school. These small acts of regular self-love contribute to an overall greater sense of happiness and satisfaction in your daily life, reduce stress, and increase resilience and self-esteem!

Use Words of Self-Love

"Words of self-love" is the internal dialogue you are having with yourself throughout the day. It's the compliments you give yourself for something well done, the mental pep talk you tell yourself as you get dressed in the morning, or the kind words of understanding and forgiveness you whisper to yourself when you make a mistake. Positive affirmations are a great example of words of self-love.

Practice Gratitude

So many mental health professionals prescribe the practice of *gratitude* to their clients. When life becomes overwhelming, dark, and stressful, our world view can develop into a negative and pessimistic one. The act of practicing gratitude on daily basis has an amazing effect on the psyche. Many of my own clients (both men and women alike) who found themselves lost in very dark places, have reported to me that one of the best interventions I have ever assigned to them was *gratitude*. This is a simple practice that helps you to slowly adjust your world view back into a positive space (or at the very least neutral). You can accomplish this practice in multiple ways: writing in a journal, writing them on index cards, or simply saying them out loud so you can hear yourself saying them. This a great way to start or end your day. Give it a try for 2 weeks and see what you think!

Practice Your Spirituality

Spirituality and religiosity can be hot topics for some. It's important you understand that I recommend this practice to those who find it important in their lives. If you do not practice spirituality in any form, don't feel pressured to do so. For those of you who do practice a faith, make sure you keep doing it! Pray, read your sacred texts, go to your spiritual community, and engage with others- spirituality is very good for you! There have been multiple research articles that demonstrate that those who have active spiritual/religious practices are more resilient, have better post-traumatic growth (this is a good thing!), and have less mental health complications overall. Try to incorporate it daily into your life, and you'll surely be caring for your mind and soul!

* * *

By re-envisioning self-care in this way, we are better able to conceptualize how we can incorporate it affordably and realistically into our busy lives. The key to great self-care is folding regular acts of self-love into your daily life, whether through gestures or positive words. The more you do this, the more it becomes a habit, and the easier it will be. The easier it becomes, the more frequently you will do it, creating a habitual cycle that works in your favor and improves your self-esteem, mental health, and overall well-being. Another benefit is that you are modeling self-love and self-care to your child! This will help them to develop these healthy habits too, which is going to improve their emotion regulation and self-esteem. It's a win-win for everyone! If you need some ideas on easy self-care activities, you'll find a list at the back of the book. Enjoy!

13

Becoming a Wholistic Parent

It has been a long journey, but hopefully it has been informative, inspiring, and healing. Parenting is hard work, and so often we find ourselves guessing at how to go about doing it! We want to be the best parent we can be, and we want to raise children that are happy, healthy, and productive members of society one day. In short, we want them to be SUCCESSFUL in all areas of their lives. But that journey of raising successful children starts with us.

So many of us were raised with less than ideal circumstances in our own childhood. Perhaps we experienced abandonment by one or both parents, experienced death, hardship, poverty, or abuse. It's hard to know how to raise your own children when you lacked positive life experiences or healthy role models yourself.

Some of us were privileged, being raised in expensive neighborhoods, living in fancy homes, and going to the best schools. Often, however, high socioeconomic statuses don't shield us from all the ugliness the world can offer. You, too, may have experienced abuse at the hands of others you thought were there to protect you, experienced a traumatic event, experienced the loss of something beloved, or were abandoned by those you relied on most. Indeed, riches often do not save us from horror of the world.

Regardless of your circumstances, regardless of your experiences, and regardless of your own upbringing, you found yourself drawn to this book because you wanted to learn a better way. You wanted to feel more informed, more capable, and less helpless in the raising of your own children. You wanted to learn the fine art that is parenting and provide your family with a wholistic, systemic approach.

13.1 Review

Over the course of this book, we have slowly peeled back the multiple layers of the "parenting onion." Looking at each layer, we developed a fuller understanding that all the components to parenting must be considered individually but executed as a whole. Focusing solely on one part of parenting isn't effective. You must look at all the pieces at once to truly understand how each part intertwines and works with the other. In doing so, you develop a more wholistic approach to parenting.

Here's a breakdown of our journey together in each chapter:

1. We looked at a bird's-eye-view to parenting and developed a general understanding of the concept of *Wholistic Parenting*.
2. You were exposed to my parenting philosophy as a framework for parenting. It was provided to you as an example of what your own parenting philosophy might look like (and, of course, you are welcome to adopt mine).
3. Next, we scratched the surface of a huge topic: the Parent-Child relationship. We reviewed different attachment styles, how they form, and how you can begin to develop a healthy attachment with your child no matter how old they currently are.
4. You took a hard look at yourself and examined who you currently are as a parent. You learned about the 4 parenting styles and took time to recognize where you currently lie on this continuum. We reviewed the 6 items that affect your parenting and looked at *goodness of fit* with your child.
5. In this section, we dug deeper into the Parent-Child relationship, recognizing how important it really is in happy, healthy, and united families. We touched on the concept of the *Emotional Piggy Bank* and investigated 3 ways you could begin enriching your relationship with your child. Then, we took a brief look at how you can begin repairing a damaged Parent-Child relationship.

6. You received a quick rundown of child development through the different developmental stages: infancy, early childhood, middle childhood, and adolescence.
7. This is where we *really* rolled up our sleeves and began digging deeper into the psychology of it all. In this section, we looked at emotions in children and how emotions affect behavior.
8. After learning about emotions, you were ready to understand the concept of *emotion regulation*. This chapter was a mammoth, touching on the roots of emotion regulation, why some individuals have poor emotion regulation, the *Fight or Flight Response*, and the "how-to's" of coping skills.
9. Your next step was learning about a wholistic approach to discipline. I provided you with a new definition of what discipline is, and you obtained a more wholistic view of how effective discipline works. You learned about structure and routine, rules and limits, and rewards and consequences. I also helped you to understand the subtle differences between bribing versus rewarding and consequences versus punishment. We broke down the 3 parts to parental consistency, learned 8 tips to effective communication with your kids, reviewed 4 tips for effective *praise*, and investigated the structure of disciplinary sessions.
10. In this section, we defined the individuals who should be considered as *co-parents*, lamented over the difficul-

ties that co-parenting can bring, and discussed how to prevent co-parenting disasters.
11. We reviewed your marriage and how children can unintentionally cause dissention in your romantic relationships. Then, we looked at 4 tips to keeping your marriage happy and healthy while raising kids.
12. Our last stop was a discussion of parental burnout, a very real, negative side-effect to parenting. We not only reviewed how parental burnout can happen but looked at how you can treat AND prevent parental burnout!

Hopefully, you can now see how each part interweaves with the other and needs to be considered and executed as a whole (i.e. *Wholistic* Parenting!).

At the beginning of this book, I informed you that you wouldn't walk away with specific parenting techniques for discipline and such. Although I provided many tips (and *yes*, I couldn't help but provide *some* parenting interventions), my main goal was for you to have a deeper, more foundational understanding of parenting.

In the beginning, I likened parenting to cooking. I explained how, being given a recipe for any dish does not make you a chef (or even a good cook!). In order to truly become a chef, you must understand the mechanics and science of cooking. You must understand the *art* of being a chef. In a similar way, teaching you parenting interventions and/or techniques is like giving you a recipe. It's only good for that one thing. It doesn't make you a better parent at your core, it doesn't help you really understand what is going on with your child, and it certainly doesn't help you understand how to adapt "the recipe" when something isn't working.

That's why you must learn the **gestalt** of it all. You must learn how each part works and how each part connects to the other, creating a fabulous system that moves together, creating the **family system**. That was the goal of this book, to help you see that bigger, bird's-eye-view, to help you adopt a wholistic parenting approach to your own family, and to help you understand the fine art that is parenting. I hope that you got that from this book, even if only a little bit. Because even a little movement in the direction of becoming a more wholistic parent will do wonders in helping you achieve a happier, more loving, and more united family in the long run. That is what I want for you.

13.2 One Small Step

It has been a long journey without a doubt, and hopefully a productive one for you. And after a long journey, we find ourselves always asking the following question:

What do I do now?

The answer is a simple one: you take one small step. Every journey begins with one small step, one small movement in the direction you hope to go. Wholistic Parenting can be incredibly overwhelming... there's just so much to consider at any given time. I've been teaching Wholistic Parenting for years, and *I* even felt overwhelmed when I was trying to write this book. It's ok to feel this way, but that's why you need to start with just one small step.

Throughout the book, I made suggestions of things that you could begin applying to your parenting today, but to try and apply them all at once can overwhelm you. This, in turn, will increase the likelihood that you won't follow through with it and eventually fail. None of us want that.

To help you be more successful, I took the time to create a companion workbook. It summarizes each chapter for you but provides additional activities and action steps for each section. It's a true guide for this journey, and it's there to help you achieve your goal more successfully. The key to changing behavior and developing new habits is to break the journey down into manageable, baby steps, and the workbook does this for you, which can be incredibly stress relieving and helpful to the busy parent.

Take one small step today. Pick one thing that you want to do differently and start doing that every single day. If you need someone to help keep you accountable, ask a friend or your co-parent to help you out. Don't be overwhelmed by it all; just pick one small step and take it! Remember, this isn't a race, and you aren't competing with anyone. This is a journey of self-growth. You are on the journey of evolving into the best version of your parenting-self, so enjoy it!

13.3 Final Thoughts

I truly love helping people; it's why I became a marriage and family therapist. But parenting is my passion, and that's why it became my specialty. I look forward to writing more books that help parents adopt a wholistic parenting approach, and I plan to continue the *Art of Parenting* series with more specific topics, such as parenting through divorce, parenting teens, and so on. As such, I would love to hear from you!

If you have a topic that you would like me to write about, you can always visit my website at kcdreisbach.com and send me a message with your suggestions. Once you are on the website, you can check out the various parenting articles I've written, covering topics such as parenting children with ADHD, Postpartum Depression, and more, available for you to access at no cost. You can also sign up for my monthly newsletter so that you know when the next book in the series comes out.

***

It has been a great pleasure guiding you in this journey. Once again, I hope you find yourself motivated in becoming the best parent that you can be! You deserve to have a happy, loving life and parenting should be something that adds to that life in a positive way. It shouldn't be a heartache. Hopefully this book has given you the roadmap to that life.

Happy Parenting!

Appendix A

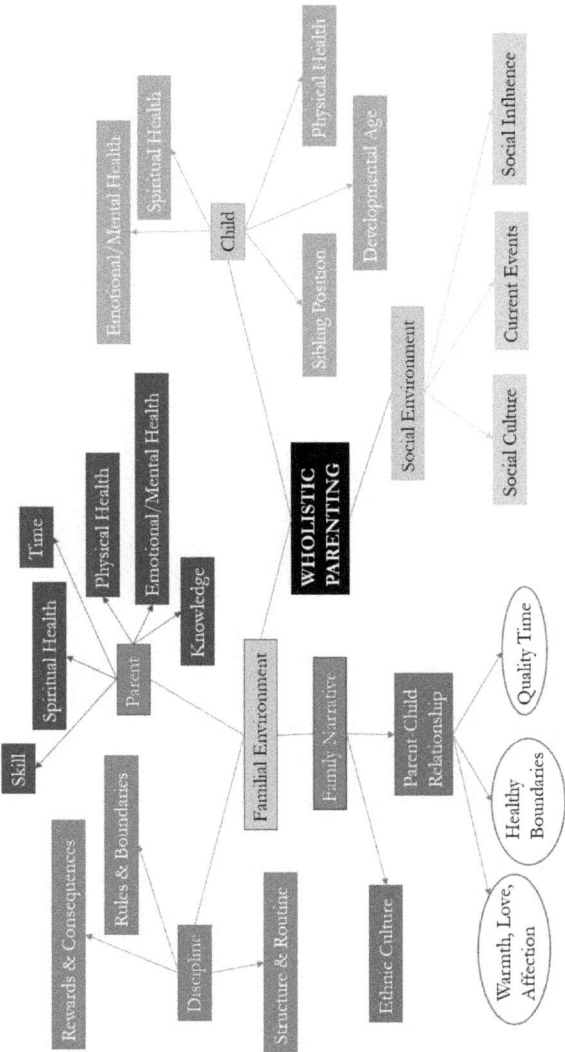

Wholistic Parenting Map
K.C. Dreisbach, LMFT

Appendix B

Enjoy this list of 50 different ideas for engaging in self-care and stress relief. There are more choices than just the ones listed, but I wanted to show you ideas that shouldn't cost you any extra money out of your pocket. Try to apply a few ideas throughout the week. For simpler ideas, such as journaling, try to apply it daily for optimum stress relief.

1. Journaling
2. Keeping a gratitude journal
3. Painting
4. Sculpting
5. Dancing
6. Working out at the gym
7. Enjoying a special treat or drink
8. Going for a walk
9. Going for a hike
10. Going for a bike ride
11. Swimming
12. Going for a drive in the car
13. 10 minutes of quiet time or napping
14. Practicing Deep Breathing/Belly Breathing
15. Progressive Muscle Relaxation
16. Taking a shower
17. Taking a bubble bath
18. Reading a book

19. Reading a magazine
20. Doing a puzzle
21. Doing a logic puzzle or word search
22. Playing a video game
23. 10 minutes surfing the web
24. Completing Grounding exercises
25. Meditating
26. Stretching exercises
27. Practicing mindfulness
28. Giving yourself a manicure or pedicure
29. Practicing yoga poses
30. Going to sleep 10 minutes early
31. Sleeping in by 10 minutes
32. Watch a movie
33. Watch an episode of your favorite TV show
34. Call a friend
35. Listen to music
36. Play an instrument
37. Sing
38. Practicing positive affirmations
39. Practice self-forgiveness
40. Having a picnic
41. Listen to an audiobook during long commutes
42. If you have a pet, taking 5-10 minutes to play with it
43. Going for a run
44. Write poetry
45. Read poetry
46. Bake or cook something enjoyable
47. Garden
48. Do photography

49. Take 5-10 minutes to look at photo-books of pleasant memories
50. Read motivational essays or books

Glossary

Ambivalent/Resistant Attachment- A pattern in which an infant shows distress before a caregiver leaves them, is significantly upset while the caregiver is absent, and then wants and resists contact with their caregiver when the caregiver returns
(Paplia and Feldman 214)

Attachment- A mutual, long-standing bond between two people (particularly between a caregiver and infant) that defines the quality of the relationship (Paplia and Feldman 213)

Authoritarian Parenting Style- A parenting style that is primarily characterized around control and obedience (Paplia and Feldman 301)

Authoritative Parenting Style- A parenting style that honors a child's individuality but balances it with social constraints. Good behavior is demanded with consistent firm standards, but balanced with love and acceptance (Paplia and Feldman 301)

Avoidant Attachment- A pattern of behavior where an infant rarely cries or fusses when they are separated from a caregiver, and then avoids contact or interaction with this caregiver when he/she returns to the infant (Paplia and Feldman 214)

Behavioral Activation- A therapeutic intervention that involve getting the client more engaged and active with pleasurable activities that have the potential to improve the individual's mood (Hindman, *Behavioral Activation*)

Big Five Factors of Personality- The 5 dimensions that many psychologists have determined personality is comprised of: openness, emotional stability, extraversion, agreeableness, and conscientiousness

Co-Parent- Those individuals who are responsible for watching your children a significant amount of the time

Conscientious Parenting- Parenting when you are in control of your emotions. Your words and actions are thought out carefully, and your interactions with your child have purpose and meaning to them.

Coping Skills- Different actions an individual can take in order to help them manage difficult emotions such as anger, anxiety, or sadness

Development- A pattern of biological, cognitive, and socioemotional processes that begins when a person is conceived and spans throughout the years of his/her life (Santrock 28)

Difficult Child- A temperament style where the child has intense emotional reactions, often negative and aggressive in nature. Children with this temperament lack self-control and are slow to accept new experiences (Santrock 136)

Discipline- Techniques used to shape a child's character and behavior. These techniques teach self-control and encourage acceptable behavior (Paplia and Feldman 298)

Disciplinary Session- When and how you engage in disciplining your child

Disorganized/Disoriented Attachment- A behavioral pattern in which an infant (after being left alone by the caregiver) will show different, contradictory behaviors when the caregiver returns (Paplia and Feldman 214)

Easy Child- A temperament style where the child has mild reactions, often positive and well-humored in nature. Children with this temperament are often in a good mood, quickly adapt to new experiences, and easily settle into regular routines (Santrock 136)

Emotion Regulation- The process by which a person manages their emotions

Emotional Piggy Bank- Analogy used to explain how relationships work

Ethnic Culture- A family's connection to their ethnicity and the related characteristics, spiritual beliefs, language, customs, and cultural heritage that the family follows and adheres too

External Coping Skills- Coping skills that exist outside of yourself or require a physical object to work, such as a stress ball

Familial Environment- This consists of your home and the multiple parts that go with it, such as each family member.

Familial Stress- All of the stressful events, interactions, and experiences that cause you stress within your family and household

Family Narrative- The story of your family, as told by any given person in your family.

Family System- A conceptual understanding of the family unit in which the family is a connected system comprised of multiple individual parts that function together (Nichols 461)

Fight or Flight Response- "Response to an acute threat to survival that is marked by physical changes, including nervous and endocrine changes, that prepare a human or an animal to react or to retreat" (Editors of Encyclopaedia Britannica)

Frustration Tolerance- This is the ability to adapt and overcome challenges, obstacles, and other stressors (Esposito, *Frazzled*)

Gestalt- "A configuration or pattern of elements so unified as a whole that its properties cannot be derived from a simple summation of its parts" ("Gestalt," def. 1)

Goodness of Fit- When the parental and environmental demands of a child's environment matches the child's temperament and ability to meet those demands (Paplia and Feldman 211)

Individuation- The normal process by which an individual struggles for autonomy and personal identity separate from other people (Paplia and Feldman 455)

Indulgent Parenting Style- A style of parenting that allows children to govern their own activities as much as possible. Discipline is infrequent, and parents are typically warm, noncontrolling, and indulgent (Santrock 77). See also *Permissive Parenting Style.*

Internal Coping Skills- Coping skills that utilize nothing but yourself, such as Deep Breathing

Layering Coping Skills- The act of using one skill, then the next, over and over again until you have regained control of your emotions

Love Maps- John Gottman's term for the all the information you have stored in your brain about your partner and their life (Gottman and Silver 48)

Microcosm- "A small, representative system having analogies to a larger system in constitution, configuration, or development" (The American Heritage Dictionary 535)

Modeling- The act of showing your children how to act and react in any given situation by a role model and acting in the desired way yourself

Natural Anxiety- The normal, healthy level of anxiety existent in all people

Nature vs Nurture- *Nature* refers to the biological, genetic make-up of a person, whereas *nurture* refers to the interactions the person had with their parents as they grew up

Neglectful Parenting Style- A style characterized by a lack of involvement. These parents rarely spend quality time with their children, know little about their children, and they fail to provide structure and/or healthy boundaries (Santrock 77)

Parent-Child Relational Triangle- When a child has been brought into the relational problems between parents. *Example: A father complains to a child about the mother's actions.*

Parent-Child Relationship- The essential bond and connection you have with your child

Parental Consistency- Parenting in the same way between all children in the home, from day to day, and in a similar way to your co-parent

Parental Sabotage- When someone undermines your parenting

Permissive Parenting Style- A parenting style that in which children govern most of their own activities. Power lies primarily with the children, and discipline is seldom used. Parents who utilize this style are often warm in nature, indulgent, demand little (if anything) from their children, and are noncontrolling (Paplia and Feldman 301). See also *Indulgent Parenting Style.*

Personality- A mixture of emotions, thoughts, temperament, and behaviors that remain consistent over time. This mixture is what makes each person unique in who they are and how they interact with the world (Paplia and Feldman 204)

Quality Time- Spending time engaging in an activity that the other person enjoys

Reactive Parenting- Whenever you are parenting from an emotional state (namely when you are angry)

Secure Attachment- A pattern in which an infant is able to to find comfort from their caregiver easily and effectively in the face of a stressful situation (Paplia and Feldman 214)

Slow-to-Warm-Up Child- A temperament style in which the child displays low emotional intensity. These children struggle to adapt, are somewhat negative, and display low levels of activity (Santrock 136)

Social Culture- The related characteristics, spiritual beliefs, languages, customs, and cultural heritage of the society in which a family lives

Social Environment- This is the outside world that your family lives in. It consists of your neighborhood, social networks, country, and current events.

Social Influence- This consists of the people that might influence you or your child.

Tantrum (Temper Tantrum)- "A fit of bad temper" (The American Heritage Dictionary 837)

Temperament- A person's style of managing life situations (Paplia and Feldman 209)

Triangulation- The process of pulling a third person into a relational conflict to help ease tension rather than managing the conflict in the original pair (Gilbert 74)

Wholistic- "The philosophy that all parts of a thing are interconnected. In medicine, wholistic treatment is the treatment of a person as a whole, mind, body and social factors" (The Grammarist Team, *Wholistic and holistic*)

Wholistic Discipline- A component to the Wholistic Parenting approach; consists of punishment, rewards, praise, structure, consistency, healthy boundaries, love and affection, rules and limits

Wholistic Parenting- Considering the mind, body, and social environment of your family and shaping your parenting to those factors

References

Amsel, Beverly. *Individuation.* 6 September 2019. 2 August 2020. www.goodtherapy.org/learn-about-therapy/issues/individuation.

"Bribe, *Verb.*" *Lexico Dictionary,* Oxford University Press; Dictionary.com. 2020. www.lexico.com/en/definition/bribe.

Chess, S and A Thomas. "Temperamental Individuality from Childhood to Adolescence." *Journal of Child Psychiatry* 16 (1977): 218-226.

"Consequence, *Noun 1.*" *Lexico Dictionary,* Oxford University Press; Dictionay.com. 2020. www.lexico.com/definition/consequence.

DeRaad, B. "The trait-coverage of emotional intelligence." *Personality & Individual Differences* 2005: 673-687.

Dreisbach, K.C. *Trials of the Working Parent: A busy mom's guide to kids, work & loving yourself.* Covina: K.C. Dreisbach, LMFT, 2019.

Editors of Encyclopaedia Brtannica. "Fight-or-flight response." *Britannica.* Encyclopaedia Britannica, Inc. 12 August 2019, www.britannica.com/science/fight-or-flight-response.

Esposito, Linda. *Frazzled: High anxiety and low frustration tolerance.* 28 November 2017. www.psychologytoday.com/us/blog/anxiety-zen/201711/frazzled-high-anxiety-and-low-frustration-tolerance.

"Gestalt, *Noun 1.*" *The American Heritage Dictionary.* New York: Houghton Mifflin Company, 2001, p. 358.

Gilbert, Roberta M. *Extraordinary Relationships: A New Way of Thinking about Human Interactions.* New York: John Wiley & Sons, Inc, 1992.

Good Therapy. *Triangulation.* 1 August 2016. 2 August 2020. www.goodtherapy.org/blog/psychpedia/triangulation.

Gottman, John and Nan Silver. *The Seven Principles for Making Marriage Work.* New York: Three Rivers Press, 1999.

Hindman, Robert. *Behavioral Activation Tip.* 21 February 2018. beckinstitute.org/behavioral-activation-tip/.

Lee, K., M.C. Ashton and K-H Shin. "Personality Correlates of Workplace Anti-Social Behavior." *Applied Psychology: An International Review* n.d.: 81-97.

Lieberman, Alicia F. *The Emotional Life of the Toddler.* New York: Simon & Schuster, 2018.

Mayo Clinic. *Healthy Lifestyle: Stress Management.* 2020. 2 August 2020. www.mayoclinic.org/healthy-lifestyle/stress-management/in-depth/stress/art-20046037.

McCrae, R.R. and P.T. Costa. *Personality in Adulthood.* 2nd. New York: Guilford, 2003.

"Microcosm, *Noun 1."The American Heritage Dictionary.* New York: Houghton Mifflin Company, 2001, p. 535.

Miller-Karas, Elaine. *Building Resilience to Trauma: The trauma and community resiliency models.* New York: Routledge, 2015

Miller-Karas, Elaine and Laurie Leitch. *Trauma Resiliency Model Workbook.* 2013.

Nichols, Michael P. *Family Therapy: Concepts and Methods.* Boston: Allyn & Bacon, 2010.

Paplia, Diane E and Ruth Duskin Feldman. *A Child's World: Infancy through Adolescence.* New York: McGraw-Hill, 2011.

"Philosophy, *2.b*" *Oxford American Dictionary and Thesaurus,* Oxford University Press, 2003, p.1121.

"Punishment, *Noun 1.*" *Lexico Dictionary,* Oxford University Press; Disctionary.com. 2020. www.lexico.com/definition/punishment.

"Reward, *Noun 1.*" *Lexico Dictionary,* Oxford University Press; Disctionary.com. 2020. www.lexico.com/definition/reward.

Santrock, John W. *Educational Psychology.* 3rd. McGraw-Hill Companies, Inc, 2008.

Selva, Joaquin. *Behavioural Activation: Behavioural Therapy for Depression Treatment.* 8 July 2020. 2 August 2020. positivepsychology.com/behavioural-activation-therapy-treating-depression/.

"Tantrum, *Noun 1.*" *The American Heritage Dictionary.* New York: Houghton Mifflin Company, 2001, p.837.

Grammarist. *Wholistis and holistic.* 24 April 2020. grammarist.com/spelling/wholistic-and-holistic/.

More by K.C. Dreisbach

Eliminating Temper Tantrums: 4 Keys to Mastering Your Child's Anger Outbursts

Trials of the Working Parent: A Busy Mom's Guide to Kids, Work & Loving Yourself

The Art of Parenting Workbook: How to Parent from Infancy to Adulthood

ABOUT THE AUTHOR

Krystal Dreisbach is a licensed marriage and family therapist, international author, and parenting expert. Her specialties include trauma, depression, anxiety, and parenting. She is the author of several books and in the founder of The Wholistic Family Blog. She completed her graduate training at Loma Linda University School of Behavioral Health where she earned her master's of science in Marital & Family Therapy.

Ms. Dreisbach resides in the greater Los Angeles area, where she owns a private practice, providing mental health services and clinical supervision. She is a member of the California Association for Marriage and Family Therapist, and a former member of the American Association for Marriage and Family Therapists. She offers psychotherapy and parenting services to clients in the greater Los Angeles, CA area, and throughout the state of California through her telehealth private practice.

www.ingramcontent.com/pod-product-compliance
Ingram Content Group UK Ltd.
Pitfield, Milton Keynes, MK11 3LW, UK
UKHW041006220326
11408UKWH00001B/24

9 780578 739854